SYMBOLS AND ZEN

Portraying the Process of Awakening

TAIZEN DALE VERKUILEN

Firethroat Press

Copyright 2025 © by Taizen Dale Verkuilen
All rights reserved

Published by Firethroat Press
Madison, WI

Email: firethroatpress@gmail.com

ISBN: 979-8-9925213-0-6

Symbols and Zen: Portraying the Process of Awakening /
Taizen Dale Verkuilen.

Includes bibliographical references.

1. Zen Buddhism. 2. Zen Buddhism--Philosophy. 3.
Introspection. 4. Awakening—

Edited by Shōkū Karin Jacobson
Book Cover by Elaine Meszaros
Book Design by Kira Henschel

Symbols and Zen:

Portraying the Process of Awakening

*"The discriminating mind is a dancer and a magician
with the objective world as his stage.
Intuitive-mind is the wise jester who travels with the magician,
and reflects upon his emptiness and transiency."* [1]
Shakyamuni Buddha in the Lankavatara Sutra

NOTE TO THE READER

A number of years ago my wife Renshin Barbara and I were writing a book together entitled *Tending the Fire: An Introspective Guide to Zen Awakening.* During the course of writing, she indicated that a symbol would be short-cut method of imparting the relationship between the the newly devised Resolution Sequence and the Yogacara teachings of the process of awakening. She declared, "Why don't you make one for us?" I spent a few days getting the basics in line, presented the outcome to her, and after a few more days of communal skullduggery, the basic symbols surfaced out of the darkness. We finished the book with the symbols at the center and with a minimal of explanation of the symbols' origins. This book attempts to overcome that gap, describing the background inspirations.

Introduction

*"Mahamati, you and all the Bodhisattva-Mahasattvas
should avoid the erroneous reasonings of the philosophers
and seek this self-realization of Noble Wisdom."* [2]
Shakyamuni Buddha in the Lankavatara Sutra

The Buddha Dharma has been changed many times by its encounters with various cultures. However, even though the forms changed radically, the essential teaching was preserved. A prime example of this is the adaptation of Indian forms of Buddhism, and the Ch'an methods developed during the creative T'ang dynasty in China. We are fortunate in the West today that most schools of Buddhism are represented in an unprecedented fashion. More than likely, one can find a center or temple in the United States for almost any form of Buddhism now practiced in the world. Nevertheless, Buddhist principles call for cultivation of imaginative activity to mold their practice forms to Western ethos.

Since the mid-twentieth century, Zen Buddhist teaching methods have been evolving by necessity as Westerners take up its practice. The twentieth-century pioneer missionary monks used their knowledge and energy to find resourceful ways to overcome the intellectual, linguistic, and cultural barriers between East and West. This book attempts to build on their efforts to clarify the basic concepts and experience, and to provide an inclusive means to adapt the teaching forms into our culture of college, family life, scientific education, and corporate employment. These new forms of study require increased flexibility in order to capture and cultivate the dynamic process of Zen Buddhist awakening for primarily lay practitioners within their fast-paced lives.

Symbols and Zen: Portraying the Process of Awakening presents a practice model that combines synergetic Yogacara Buddhism with the Resolution Sequence, an adaptation of David Grove's groundbreaking psycho-linguistic Metaphor Therapy. Both Yogacara and the Resolution Sequence teach a means of

1

transformation based on accessing and employing intuitive information uncontaminated by interpretation by either the teacher or disciple. This blended model offers creative means of understanding and fulfilling the process of awakening.

YOGACARA BUDDHISM

Shakyamuni Buddha taught for forty-five years after his awakening. During his teaching career he taught on many levels. After his death these levels were categorized into what we know as The Three Turnings of the Wheel of Dharma.

In the First Turning, the Buddhist practitioner undertakes an analysis of the self and its constituents in order to understand the functioning of the self and to resolve the conditioned states at the root of suffering. Conceptual understanding of the mind's elements and functions is at the heart of its method.

The Second Turning teaches the direct experience of the emptiness of reality, apart from conceptual mediation, and views the conceptual basis of the First Turning as incomplete understanding.

The Third Turning of Yogacara Buddhism arose because of the necessity to resolve the seeming conflict between the personal approach of the First Turning, and the universal experience of the Second. The Third Turning focuses on the complementary relationship of concept and immediacy. We are creatures of both thought and experience, made whole in the experiential understanding of their intimate relationship.

The Third Turning facilitates the inner dialogue between the dualistic pairs of our makeup. The unified approach of Yogacara Buddhist teaching embodies the threefold process of awakening: resolving conditioned states, integrating the freedom from conditioned states, and living that freedom. Yogacara Buddhism initiates action through an introspective analysis into the operation and resolution of conditioned states that removes the obstructions inhibiting the inner dialogue between the Personal and Universal Aspects of Mind.

2

Yogacara comprehends the equal importance of the Personal and Universal Aspects of Mind; practitioners must understand their makeup and functioning and the nature of their relationship. Practitioners who develop the Personal Mind without the Universal Mind are deprived of the fullness of insight and their orientation tends toward the moralistic and scholastic. In the absence of the Personal Mind, the Universal Mind stands apart from the resolution of conditioned states, and the source of their associated afflictive emotions remains deeply rooted in the storehouse consciousness.[3] The concepts of the Personal without the experiential intuitions of the Universal offer fragments as answers; the intuitions of the Universal without the concepts of the Personal are without an established base.

RESOLUTION SEQUENCE

The Resolution Sequence accomplishes a very similar objective as Yogacara through an introspective guide, employing an inquiry-response activity analogous to the *mondo* give-and-take between a master and disciple.[4] The Resolution Sequence is a respectful and elegant process by which we can define a conditioned state with purposeful and focused attention. Through a precise and nonintrusive method of investigation, intuitive information arises and gives form and clarity to a practitioner's psychophysical landscape.

Working in this manner allows us to interact with our internal processes in ways that descriptive explanations do not allow. The process of the Resolution Sequence is mysterious and incomprehensible to our ordinary perspective, yet intriguing enough to engage our full and necessary cooperation. The Resolution Sequence, like Zazen, allows direct participation with the wisdom of the Universal Mind through our active attention.

SYMBOLIC REPRESENTATION

In this book, we will formulate a series of symbols that encapsulate Yogacara and the Resolution Sequence teachings. We will "grow" the symbols piece by piece, with Shakyamuni Buddha's "how to gain Noble Wisdom" teaching of the Lankavatara Sutra as the basis and background. In the Lankavatara Sutra, Buddha explains the steps leading to realization by incorporating Mahayana and Yogacara teachings. Quotations from the sutra are placed in chapter headings and other locations as the guiding concepts for creation of the symbols. (The reader is advised to download a copy of the sutra and read the introduction to gain a basic understanding of its origination and relation to the Yogacara concepts used extensively in the text. See footnote for download information.)[5]

Symbols are effective in condensing and transmitting large amounts of information and instructions in concise forms. They have been instrumental in many fields of creative activity providing means of documentation and pathways of development. A significant example of how the use of symbols brought enormous change occurred in the field of mathematics in the seventeenth century. Uncomplicated symbolic expressions replaced convoluted rhetorical terms and in time opened the field to an unexcelled period of ingenuity and practical application.

The use of symbols is similar to the replacement in mathematics of the awkward rhetorical steps, presenting a symbolic expedient of self-discovery, one "free from the domination of words."[6] Symbolic display of the essence of Buddha's instructions simplifies the approach to learning, refining, and implementing the fundamental processes of awakening.

****

This book consists of six chapters that develop the basic symbols along with a grammar of awakening. It also includes an appendix that demonstrates how the symbols can be employed in simplifying the study of other Buddhist teachings.

CHAPTER 1
THE VALUE OF SYMBOLS IN MATHEMATICS
Chapter 1 supplies examples and descriptions of the change from the rhetorical to symbols in mathematics. Mathematics symbols provide

a good comparison, because all of us learned the grammar of algebra step-by-step. Learning and applying the grammar of awakening requires a similar process. The examples provide a firm foundation of understanding for how symbols influenced the growth of mathematics. The chapter begins the analysis of how a comparable grammar of awakening may be as equally viable in the practice of Zen.

CHAPTER 2
FIRST STEPS TOWARD A GRAMMAR OF AWAKENING
The introductory quotation from the Lankavatara Sutra at the beginning of the chapter offers Buddha's guidance for the generation of the grammar of awakening. The definitions of the basic Buddhist concepts will be used as the basis in later chapters during the development of symbols.

CHAPTER 3
FIRST MAGNIFICATION – THE SYMBOL OF NONDUALITY
The insight of Zazen supplies the understanding to create six symbols that depict the stages for understanding Buddha's statement, "I teach the nature of *dukkha* and its cessation." Each symbol distills the insights from a cluster of basic teachings into a clear statement in the grammar of awakening.

CHAPTER 4
SECOND MAGNIFICATION – THE NONDUALITY–RESOLUTION SEQUENCE SYMBOL
Adding the introspection of the Resolution Sequence to the Symbol of Nonduality presents an expansive view of the process of awakening. The second magnification, powered by the Resolution Sequence, produces six additional symbols that capture the deepening levels of the knowledge and resolution of conditioned states.

CHAPTER 5
SYMBOLS AND THE GRAMMAR OF AWAKENING

This chapter summarizes the symbolic and verbal representations of the grammar of awakening developed in Chapters 3 and 4. The chapter also includes a description of what the Lankavatara Sutra terms the "faculty of intuition" and its functioning.

CHAPTER 6
WHAT HAVE WE LEARNED

Chapter 6 attempts to answer questions conceived in Chapter 1 regarding the efficacy of the use of symbols in Buddhist practice.

APPENDIX

The appendix contains four introductory approaches to Buddhist teachings using the symbols developed in the text.

DUKKHA AND CONDITIONED STATES

There are two major topics of discussion in this book that require explanation before we start because they are important for foundational understanding. The subjects are *dukkha* and conditioned states. These items have been clarified in our book *Tending the Fire: An Introspective Guide to Zen Awakening*. Additional definition will be provided after brief excerpts from *Tending the Fire*.

"The term for this suffering in Buddhism is *dukkha*; it has three major components: ordinary suffering, impermanence, and conditioned states. The first cause of *dukkha* is the physical and mental pain that beings experience. It includes all the ways we suffer due to physical illness or incapacity, as well as mental suffering. The second cause of *dukkha* is that the nature of reality is impermanence. Although that may give one hope in difficult times because one can count on the fact that things will change, it causes suffering when pleasant times turn troublesome. The third cause of *dukkha* is conditioned states. Conditioned states are deeply rooted psychophysical formations predicated by negative experiences, and they are how we store negative learning. They arise as a way to mitigate difficult life events, but continue to influence our experience and behavior long after an event is over."[7]

"Conditioned states cause afflictive emotions and are the one aspect of *dukkha* we can actively work to resolve. *Tending the Fire* is dedicated and this text as well to exploring conditioned states and their intimate relationship to awakening. It is the position of this work that conditioned states can and should be worked on directly as a central concern in the process of awakening."[8]

PERSONAL AND UNIVERSAL ASPECTS OF MIND

The terms Personal Mind and Universal Mind were chosen over the often-used terminology of Relative and Absolute, Apparent and Real, Conventional and Ultimate, etc. for three reasons:

1. Personal and Universal more accurately describe the intimate relationship that exists between the two aspects of mind. The complementary interplay between the Personal and Universal Aspects of Mind, as well as all other dualities, is one of subtle closeness, an attribute not fully conveyed by abstract expressions.

2. Buddha uses the terms Personal and Universal in the Lankavatara Sutra quotations that are liberally spread throughout the book.

3. I want to be consistent with our other writings, where we've used the terms in this way.

Chapter 1
The Value of Symbols in Mathematics

THE EXPLOSION OF THE USE OF SYMBOLS
During the fifteenth, sixteenth, and seventeenth centuries mathematics made an imaginative leap, evolving from a system anchored in a perplexing rhetoric as the method of defining problems, to one of inclusive and clarifying symbolic expressions. Greco-Roman mathematical texts became available during that time showing that the replacement of complex linguistic definitions with letter symbolism began in classical times. A number of Renaissance European mathematicians, following the leads of their predecessors, devised letter-based systems, but it was the notational scheme of René Descartes, largely based on the work of the English mathematician Thomas Hariott, that drew the most attention. Among other innovations, he reserved the letters of the alphabet for unknowns and variables. Descartes had wide influence, and the mathematical community largely adopted his system because of its accuracy and ease of use.

The author E. T. Bell described the process of replacement of words with symbols in his book *The Development of Mathematics* as follows: "an incredible mass of confusing terminology and inefficient rules was swept into the past, and with it an equal or greater mass of tortuous thinking."[10] High school students often consider present-day word problems as bewildering. Can you imagine how much worse the situation would be today without symbols? Descartes and his colleagues saved us from having to cope with the "tortuous" rhetorical expressions.

EFFECTS OF THE EXPLOSION

Mathematics benefited in at least five major ways by jettisoning rhetorical definitions, while simultaneously accepting and cultivating the use of symbols in their place.

- Simplification of the problem statement
- Facilitation of problem solving
- Provision of a basis for continuous innovative change
- Creation of symbolic forms to inspire and refine ideas
- Expansion of the ability to communicate knowledge and learning

This list of benefits shows how symbolization improved mathematics. Mathematics grew from an arcane endeavor into a universal force penetrating all of science and much of world culture. The universal use of symbols in mathematics supplies a powerful means to simplify mathematical education. In addition, it offers a coherent language that supports communication and collaboration within scientific research. Before symbols gained pervasive authority in mathematics, it was a subject of great interest for a few; afterward it became a discipline of great power for many.

- Can symbolizing Buddhist teachings have similar effects on Sangha development?
- Could symbols simplify and facilitate the study of the Zen awakening process, removing the notion that awakening is only possible for monks and specialists who are able to dedicate their lives to its pursuit?
- Can symbolic notation that graphically depicts the existential process of awakening come to be as technically and intellectually effective in Buddhism as symbols are in mathematics?

Before we can answer questions like these, the necessary groundwork must be in place. We will start with a survey of the five identified benefits of symbolic notation, of how mathematics improved and delivered practical benefits to society at large and of a

9

possible relationship of Zen and symbolic notation.

SIMPLIFICATION OF THE PROBLEM STATEMENT

The first and most essential element of problem solving is to identify the problem. Saying that seems foolish, but many good intentions have crumbled under the weight of feeble clarity at the onset. Understanding symbolism's ability to overcome this basic shortcoming removed many a frown.

Each symbol cuts innumerable words and explanations, and communicates a broad understanding of concepts embedded in the symbol's definitions and placement in the equation. The lexicon of mathematical symbols reduces complicated and obscure propositions into simpler step-by-step processes. Before symbolic notation, a complex series of descriptions unique to each individual problem described the sought-for unknown factor. Symbolic notation often allows the immediate definition of the unknown factor as seen in the following illustration.

The Greek mathematician Diophantus' tombstone poses an algebra puzzle that caused a great deal of head scratching for his contemporaries (250 CE).

"Here lies Diophantus the wonder behold.
Through the art of algebraic, the stone tells how old:
God gave him a boyhood one-sixth of his life.
One twelfth more as a youth while his whiskers grew rife;
And then one-seventh ere marriage begun;
In five years, there came a bounding new son.
Alas the child of master and sage
Passed on after attaining half measure his father's full age.
After consoling his fate with the science of numbers,
Then four years later came final slumber."[11]

With modern symbols and an intuitive understanding of the grammar of algebra, many grade school scholars would have little trouble quickly establishing what is to be done and how to do it.

Let   x = unknown length of lifetime of Diophantus

     x/2 = length of son's lifetime

   1/6 x = Boyhood

  1/12 x = Youth

   1/7 x = Before Marriage

The equation therefore is

$$x = (1/6 + 1/12 + 1/7)x + x/2 + 5 + 4$$

Solving for x

$$x = 84 \text{years, length of lifetime of Diophantus}$$

Working within a defined process, the problem and its unknown are quickly identified and clearly stated, and the path to the solution is simply follows the rules of the grammar of algebra.

FACILITATION OF PROBLEM SOLVING

Symbolic notation results in a graphical representation of the problem in a form where each symbol connotes a meaning larger than its definition by its positioning in the equation. Knowing the rules and how to apply them makes symbolic manipulation possible. A symbolic path derives answers and evades Bell's "tortuous" thinking, which was the inevitable result of word-based problem definitions. Following the explicit methods of calculations defined in the grammar of algebra provides the mathematician a direct path to the problem solution.

The grammar of algebra is the underlying influence that directs the solution of the equation. Each symbol, along with its place in the equation, stands for a variable or unknown, a set of concepts, and relationships to the other symbols in the equation. When learned, the grammar of algebra becomes an unnoticed conceptual structure that directs the equation-solution process.

PROVISION OF A BASIS FOR CONTINUOUS INNOVATIVE CHANGE

In 1648 the philosopher Thomas Hobbes complained that the use of symbols would prove to be an unnecessary complication, predicting "you will not, I think, for the future be so much in love with them."[12]

It must be noted that Hobbes was not a mathematician.

On the other hand, the German mathematician Gottfried Leibniz claimed that the generation and cultivation of symbols was the key to increased comprehension not only in mathematics, but also into all matters of human thought. Excellent symbolic notation had the following value, "The true method should further us …with a sensible and palpable medium which will guide the mind."[13] Leibniz invented over 200 symbols for mathematical values and operations.

Symbols concisely arrange and convey large amounts of knowledge, much like a high-level computer programming code outstrips assembly language. Without the baggage, symbolic mathematics freed the genius of Newton, Gauss, Einstein, the innovators of Quantum Theory, as well as uncounted others who use mathematics in their daily pursuits. Solving equations is not the end of inventiveness. The mind at times may open to new ways of doing and thinking that arise from within Leibniz's "medium which will guide the mind." Mathematics energized by symbols presents new ways of formulating reflective knowledge and becomes a gateway to insight and creative thought.

CREATION OF SYMBOLIC FORMS TO INSPIRE AND REFINE IDEAS

Mathematicians enjoyed the benefits of symbolic depictions and their ability to open entirely new points of view. The new symbols swept away the cumbersome systems of notation hindering mathematics and enabled flashes of intuition. Newton acknowledged, "If I have seen further than others, it is by standing upon the shoulders of giants." The intuitional clarity found in his laws of motion and gravity stand as a tribute to the innovators of symbols, as well as a stimulus to those who followed him.

The speed and depth of mathematical development starting around 1600, a momentum that continues today faster than ever, confirms the power of symbols. The replacement of rhetorical clutter with mathematical symbols offered mathematicians a newly constituted visual that became a continuing source of ingenuity and originality. As mathematical symbols became the norm, their use facilitated communication between the personal experiences of the mathematician, and the knowledge of the world embedded in the equation.

EXPANSION OF THE ABILITY TO COMMUNICATE KNOWLEDGE AND LEARNING

Without the written word, science could not have developed into the cultural juggernaut that it is today. Similarly, without symbolic language, mathematics would have remained a sideline player rather than a central actor, offering a coherent language that probes the reality of nature providing descriptions of what it discovers in a commonly understood vocabulary. Shared notational symbols spread clarity and unity within the mathematics community, and served as an exemplar for expanded symbology in the arts and sciences.

Like the written word, each symbol has external and internal connotations. A spoken sentence has a literal meaning, and also a personal meaning for both the speaker and listener. Symbols, like words, multi-track carrying and conveying great amounts of covert information. The symbol's place in the equation defines the proper means of calculation – its literal understanding. When solving equations, mathematicians unconsciously apply the underlying world of metaphor and insight unique to their experience and knowledge.

Mathematics communicates with symbolic notation. With its newfound flexibility and innovation mathematics became the driver for growth of all the sciences. Mathematics and science have developed together along a fast trajectory for the last four centuries, with the practical applications of the sciences penetrating all aspects of our lives. Mathematics-inspired techno-science has replaced philosophy and religion as the main driver of cultural change. Hence, the expansion of symbol-based mathematics lies close to the root of the major contemporary cultural shifts.

SUMMARY

The most powerful feature of symbolic notation is opening a way to a common mental outlook. Symbols identify life's well-known and commonplace components and establish connections. In the objective world, solving an equation directs us to the desired unknown; in the inner world, mathematician's use of symbol connects them with the limitless internal space of opportunity, ideas, and creative imagery. The five ways that mathematics benefited by switching from verbal descriptions to symbolic notation offer similar improvements to Zen study. In Chapter 6, we will examine the accuracy of this assertion and answer questions raised earlier in this chapter, after developing the symbols and grammar of awakening statements.

Chapter 2
First Steps toward a Grammar of Awakening

"Transcendental Intelligence is the inner state of
self-realization of Noble Wisdom.
It is realized suddenly and intuitively as the "turning about"
that takes place in the deepest seat of consciousness."[14]
Shakyamuni Buddha in the Lankavatara Sutra

WHAT IS AWAKENING?
Awakening is the goal of Zen practice. The Buddha states awakening is the "turning about" in the deepest seat of consciousness wherein the resolution of his assertion "I teach the nature of *dukkha* and its cessation" takes place. Access to the deepest seat requires a long-term committed effort. Therefore, clear instructions detailing the process of awakening are essential. Awakening is as innate to humans as the ability to communicate verbally.

That which prevents realization is a fundamental misperception that is also innate to human experience. It is the life's default setting, naturally activated, and precisely what obstructs our inherent potential for awakening. This fundamental misperception identifies the self as a permanent entity separate from the world. Creation and application of a series of symbols presents instructions in an easily memorized graphical form, offering practitioners an orderly sequence of directions that instructs and clarifies how to approach and resolve the fundamental misperception.

WHAT IS THE GRAMMAR OF AWAKENING?
To solve algebraic equations, one must understand the assigned meanings of the symbols. The meanings and order are not objects of reflection and thought, but act "automatically" after a practitioner has thoroughly studied, understood, and memorized them as set of

guiding rules. These same requirements hold true for the process of awakening symbols as well. To create a grammar of awakening for symbols that embody the process of awakening, we must identify the underlying structure and place the symbols into relationships that match how the structures exist in the world. When they function without reflective thought, the grammar of awakening has the ability to accurately direct the three elements of the process of awakening.

In this chapter we will itemize the core Yogacara Buddhist teachings that will be embedded in the symbols.

ELEMENTS OF THE PROCESS OF AWAKENING

"The Universal Mind, cleared of its defilements
that come by effort, study, meditation,
and by gradual self-realization of Noble Wisdom,
shines forth instantaneously
with the rays that issue from its Self-nature." [15]
Shakyamuni Buddha in the Lankavatara Sutra

In the quotation above, the Buddha established three necessary ingredients for awakening. They are in essence, the teachings of the Third Turning of Yogacara Buddhism, stated in a very direct fashion: remove obstructions, seek and find intuitive insight, learn to live the truth of wisdom.

1. Resolution of defilements (*The Universal Mind, cleared of its defilements that come by effort, study, meditation*)
2. The nature and relationship of gradual and sudden awakenings (*gradual self-realization... shines forth instantaneously with the rays that issue from its Self-nature*)
3. Realization of Noble Wisdom as the fundamental component (*self-realization of Noble Wisdom*)

The following listing provides descriptions of each of these items. Expanded definitions will be developed in subsequent chapters.

1. RESOLUTION OF DEFILEMENTS
The resolution of defilements requires knowledge of the Twelve Links

of the Chain of Causation, the practice of Zazen, the Buddhist understanding of ignorance, knowledge of conditioned states, and a method to engage productively in the process of transformation.

Twelve Links of the Chain of Causation
The Twelve Links of the Chain of Causation provides a concise view of the cyclical nature of the causes and conditions that perpetuate the cycle of *dukkha*. Without conscious intervention, the Twelve Links arises and operates in our lives automatically. It begins with Ignorance and proceeds through Birth and Death, repeating itself again and again.

Buddhist understanding of ignorance
Buddhist understanding of ignorance is not an absence of knowledge. It is the fundamental misperception embedded in the personality that experiences the self as a distinct from the world. It is the source of conditioned states.

Practice of Zazen
The practice of Zazen is an information-based mental discipline that contains the means to connect with the deepest aspects of our being, where we learn to see the world free of *a priori* embellishment. Zazen practice removes obstructions, leading the practitioner to be more fully present in the world as it unfolds.

Knowledge of conditioned states
Conditioned states arise from the third type of *dukkha* (the first two are physical pain and impermanence as the nature of reality). They consist of a complex of afflictive emotions, habitual thought patterns and behaviors. They limit our freedom to respond to life in ways we might prefer until we become aware of their existence and learn how to resolve them. Effort in Zazen, combined with consciously working on conditioned states, is a vehicle for gaining liberation. It is helpful to consult these five levels of awareness when working with conditioned states.

- Acknowledgement that they exist.
- What conditioned state(s) am I aware of?
- What are their triggers?
- What afflictive emotions do they bring about?
- How do they affect internal and external relationships?

Engaging in the process of transformation

Learning and applying the sequence of steps in the process of transformation resolves and uproots conditioned states and initiates liberation.

2. THE NATURE AND RELATIONSHIP OF GRADUAL AND SUDDEN AWAKENINGS

Gradual awakenings cause changes in worldview perspectives; sudden awakenings engender changes in being and behavior. There are four awakenings within the process of transformation: the first and third are gradual, and the second and fourth can be either sudden or gradual.

- Ability to observe the operation of a conditioned state
- Resolution of a conditioned state resulting in freedom from the confinement of afflictive emotions associated with it, which is replaced by the liberation of thusness
- Ability to observe and begin the integration of the changes and to fully embody the transformative change of being
- Recognition that changes are completely integrated making responses to life natural and in accord with the needs of oneself and others

3. NOBLE WISDOM

Noble Wisdom manifests within the reality of the Dharma Seals as the three aspects of the process of awakening and as the intuitive relationship of the Personal and Universal Aspects of Mind.

The Three Dharma Seals

In Buddhist teachings, fundamental truths are characterized as universal, inevitable, true in the past, and true in the future. The Three Dharma Seals possess these ultimate qualities.

Impermanence

All phenomena are subject to birth and death without exception. Nothing remains the same. The myriad forms of the universe change constantly, unfolding in a beginningless and endless stream.

Interdependence (No self-nature, dependent origination)

All beings are an ephemeral gathering of physical and mental components, drawn together by the shared action of the universe conditioning an individual's life. The extensive actions arise from those presently living, as well as all antecedent beings. All phenomena are the result of causes and conditions; when the causes and conditions cease, the phenomena pass away.

Nirvana (Intimacy)

Nirvana means cessation of suffering. Practitioners seek Nirvana in three different ways.

- Those who seek relief from pain in an eternal resting place
- Those who seek relief in cessation of thought
- Those who shift their attention from a retreat from the external world to a conscious engagement with the all-inclusive mysteries of the subjective and objective worlds

The first two spring from and perpetuate delusive ways of thinking. The third recognizes Nirvana as the fundamental process of everything.

Three Aspects of the Process of Awakening

The three aspects of the process of awakening are resolving the *dukkha* of conditioned states, refining and integrating the freedom of Thusness, and attaining of unity.

Resolving the dukkha of conditioned states

Practitioners consciously pursue transformation. They encounter, embrace, and resolve conditioned states. The conscious efforts within the practice of Zazen transform defiled realms into spheres of wisdom and liberation.

Refining and integrating the freedom of Thusness

Refining and integrating the freedom of Thusness reveals the path to liberation from conditioned states and their associated habit energies. True Thusness works to put an end to habit energies.

Attaining unity

Attaining unity manifests as a change in behavior where awakening reflects in an authentic life of peace and equanimity.

Intuitive Relationship of the Personal and Universal Aspects of Mind

The Personal Mind consists of an individual's distinct and unique components. They are products of culture, education, nurture, volitional acts, and the immediate environment. The Universal Mind is made up of collective and ultimate characteristics, defined as the shared action of the universe conditioning an individual's life, arising from the actions of all antecedent beings from deepest antiquity. The nature of the relationship of the Personal and Universal Aspects of Mind is an all-inclusive Nonduality that exhibits characteristics that are hard to define, enigmatic, and ambiguous.

The relationship of the Personal and Universal Aspects of Mind becomes perceptible and grows within the intimate internal communication of Zen dialogue. Zen Master Dōgen calls this *Mitsugo*, a secret talk that suggests an intuitive perception, one that can be recognized and understood but has no sound. Within *Mitsugo*, the known inquiry of the Personal Mind convenes with the unknown response of the Universal. Understanding these relationships and working with them acknowledges that the Personal and Universal Aspects of Mind are of equal importance and must be understood and developed simultaneously. The two act interdependently with an equal level of consequence within a complex web of relationships.

SUMMARY

Creating the grammar of awakening establishes the behind-the-scene rules for a new language. Memorizing and then translating the basics of Buddhist thought into a grammar of awakening may seem daunting. However, when one pauses to consider and compare what was gained by learning successfully the grammar of algebra, the effort appears worthwhile. Creating a symbolic language for mathematics opened the door to a new world. The system of mathematical notation did not encumber instead it unleashed originality. Joseph Mazur, author of *Enlightening Symbols* describes the transcendental action of symbols in mathematics. If we substitute "grammar of awakening" for "symbol" in the following quote, we can begin to appreciate what symbols bring to the relationship of the Personal and Universal Aspects of Mind.

> *"The word 'symbol' suggests that, when familiar is thrown together with the unfamiliar, something new is created, Or, to put it another way, when the unconscious idea fits the conscious one, a new meaning emerges. The symbol is exactly that: meaning derived from connections of conscious and unconscious thoughts."[16]*

Beginning in the next chapter, we will methodically construct a series of symbols out of the chief components of Shakyamuni's teachings that creatively captures the essence of, "I teach the nature of *dukkha* and its cessation."

Chapter 3
First Magnification
The Symbol of Nonduality

"Between the Universal Mind and the Personal Mind
is the intuitive-mind, which is dependent upon Universal Mind
for its cause and support and enters into relation with both.
It partakes of the universality of Universal Mind, and shares its purity.
Through the intuitive-mind, the faculty of intuition,
the inconceivable wisdom of Universal Mind is revealed and made
realizable."[17]

Shakyamuni Buddha in the Lankavatara Sutra

The key to success in Zen practice lies in appreciation of the makeup and content of what the Buddha terms Noble Wisdom, also referred to as Nonduality, Dharmakaya, Nirvana, Ultimate Principle, and by many other names. The essential problem in living is our unawareness of the ever-surrounding mystery. This habitual incomplete understanding perceives life as separation rather than intimate interdependence. Breaking this unexamined pattern requires guided direction. One can seek counseling from an experienced teacher who will instruct a beginner in an introspective life designed to put an end to unconscious responses. Choosing the path of awakening, the "wisdom of Universal Mind" revealed by Buddha's "faculty of intuition" becomes the touchstone of daily life. The faculty of intuition described by the Buddha operates as the mediator between the Personal and Universal Aspects of Mind. The mediating wisdom arises from within the Universal, and is brought to awareness by the mental discipline of Zazen. The enhanced vision of Zazen reveals the truth of the Universal Mind's existence, supplying the information and guidance to form a lucid and accurate depiction of the process of awakening.

As stated earlier, the Symbol of Nonduality will be based on Buddhist thought supplemented with features that denote deeper concepts and understanding. Each geometric addition to the symbol will represent an elementary teaching that guides the process of awakening. The goal of the Symbol of Nonduality is to systematize the life of awakening, moving it from conceptual explanations and freestanding insights, using a well-defined set of sequential stages that bring into being a universal language like the one that symbols deliver in mathematics.

Twelve Links in the Chain of Causation

"The discriminations of the mind [are] perpetuated by habit-energy,
... from which they are given over to false imagination."[18]
Shakyamuni Buddha in the Lankavatara Sutra

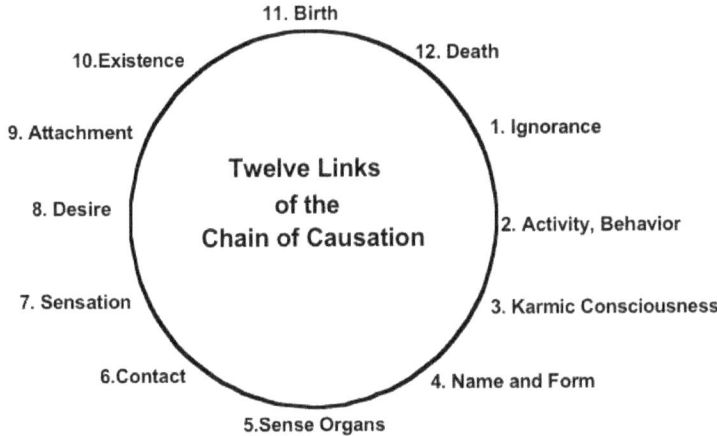

The first step in the building of a Symbol of Nonduality is illustrating the teaching of the Twelve Links of the Chain of Causation. The Twelve Links is the foundational principle of Buddhist instruction; therefore, the symbol must begin there as well, accurately rendering the cyclical nature of a life unconsciously constrained by causes and conditions. Without conscious intervention, the Twelve Links arises and operates automatically, repeating itself again and again. From the first link of Ignorance, and culminating in the eleventh and twelfth of Birth and Death, the functioning of the Twelve Links reveals a dizzying array of mental and emotional states that emerge, exist for a time, and inevitably pass on. Though the phenomena may come to an end, the underlying conditions of the Twelve Links are more basic and continue to exist. The conditions continue to function with no discernible beginning or conclusion.

The Twelve Links of the Chain of Causation is a basic explanation of dependent origination. The Twelve Links helps explain the origin of individual and collective sentient life, and how one moment connects to the next. Nothing stands alone, and no being possesses a permanent enduring self. Individual existence is always interrelated so that if one thing changes, everything is immediately affected. All beings depend on all other beings for their existence; all phenomena share an interdependent nature.

Ignorance, the first step of the Twelve Links, is the outcome of an unending stream of involuntary internal and external circumstances, and it is the source of all suffering in the world. Ignorance is not stupidity, but is rooted in an incomplete awareness of the action of cause and effect, dependent origination, and impermanence. These encumbrances impede the recognition of the possibility of awakening, trapping the unaware to repeat endless cycles around the Twelve Links.

The second link is Behavior, which is activity based on the first link of Ignorance. The Flower Ornament Sutra says, "There are two kinds of activity – the continuous generation of karmic causes and the continuous suffering resulting from the causes." The causes and conditions set in motion in Ignorance display in actions of the body, manner of speech, and quality of mental formations. If the conditioning (i. e. conditioned state, which is how an individual experiences it) is negative, and one does not recognize or does not know how to work with the negative outcomes of the conditioned state, the cycle of the Twelve Links of the Chain of Causation will proceed without any impediment to its unfavorable conclusion. The end of a cycle can be considered as the end of life, or an end of the effects of a particular set of causes and conditions within a life. In any case, a new cycle repeats, and yet another round of Ignorance commences.

For purposes of simplicity the building of the Symbol of Nonduality magnifies and symbolizes what occurs only at the encounter of the first two links of Ignorance and Behavior. The emphasis on the first two links conveys the notion that breaking the Twelve Links happens easiest at the beginning of the cycle, avoiding difficulties and complexities that arise later on.

What is the grammar of awakening for this addition?
The Twelve Links of the Chain of Causation is recognized as a fact of existence.

Understanding the Nature of Ignorance

"The mind-system, which is the most characteristic mark of personality,
originated in ignorance, …is stored in
the Universal Mind since beginning-less time,
and is still being accumulated where it conditions
the appearance of personality and its environment."[19]
Shakyamuni Buddha in the Lankavatara Sutra

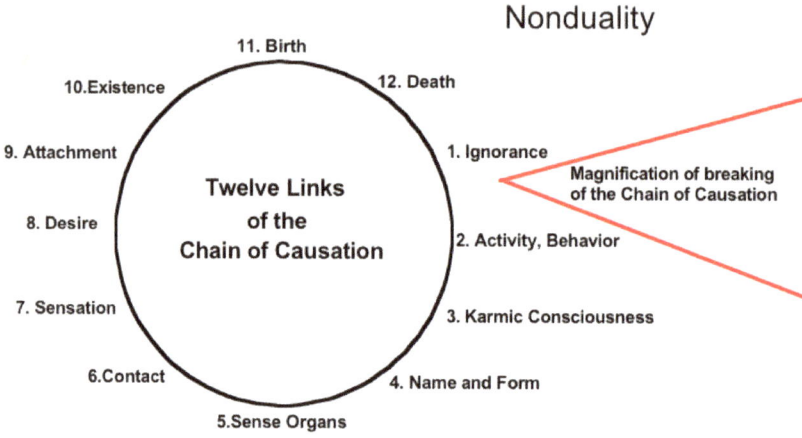

The expansion lines added to the symbol indicate a magnification of the relationship of the first link of Ignorance and the second link of Behavior. The lines of magnification are analogous to how a microscope enlarges small things into perceivable events or entities. As different types of microscopes offer varying degrees of magnification, the symbol will provide an expanded view of the many constituents and their roles within the process of awakening. For now, the lines give the first level of insight into the possibility of breaking the Twelve Links. Additions to the symbol will act like more powerful microscopes showing deeper levels of the previously imperceptible. The expansion lines symbolize increasing awareness of the conditioned states that arise from Ignorance have on Behavior. These symbols, and all subsequent symbols, illustrate deepening insight into the existence, form, nature, and functioning of conditioned states at the second stage of the Twelve Links.

The magnification begins a mindful witnessing of the mechanical process of the Twelve Links of the Chain of Causation; in our case, it focuses specifically on the interaction of the first two links. An unknown cause triggers the first link of Ignorance (storehouse consciousness), producing pleasant and afflictive outcomes in the second link of Behavior. This goes on and on without stopping. Zazen practice provides knowledge of the mental states produced by Ignorance and its influence on activity and Behavior. This nascent awareness uncovers the deep truth regarding the operation of the first two links. Ignorance is a constant stream of impulses from which afflictions arise and ripen. Observation, coupled with a fundamental awareness, replaces the previously unconscious action of the Twelve Links with an emerging knowledge of conditioned states. Experiential truth of the nature of conditioned states and their connection with afflictions takes the place of the uncertainty and perplexity of ingrained reactive responses.

Of the three kinds of *dukkha* (physical pain, impermanence as the nature of reality, and conditioned states), we are interested in conditioned states and the afflictive emotions that arise from them. Alleviation of physical pain and the effects of impermanence are possible and commendable, but temporary at best. However, conscious engagement with conditioned states can lead to their resolution and freedom. Originating in Ignorance, an unremitting flow of habitual reactions, based on a personal and unique set of causes, manifests as conditioned states. These causes can be either external events or internal stimuli. They express themselves automatically with negative emotional tones that are often considered "normal," because they have existed within us for most or all of our conscious life. Conditioned states leave a painful wake of reactive response and disharmony. No amount of well-intended willful action seems to lessen permanently their effect, let alone access its root cause. Understanding the nature of conditioned states helps us form a correct view of our existential dilemma. Zen practice has a shaky foundation without a correct view, conceptual understanding, and firsthand experience of the form and function of conditioned states.

What is the grammar of awakening for this addition?
The lines of magnification reveal the experiential reality of conditioned states.

Zazen and Nonduality

"There are four kinds of Dhyana (concentrative meditation):
The meditation practiced by beginners;
the meditation devoted to the examination of meaning;
the meditation with Thusness for its object;
and the meditation of the Buddha Tathágatas" [20]

Shakyamuni Buddha in the Lankavatara Sutra

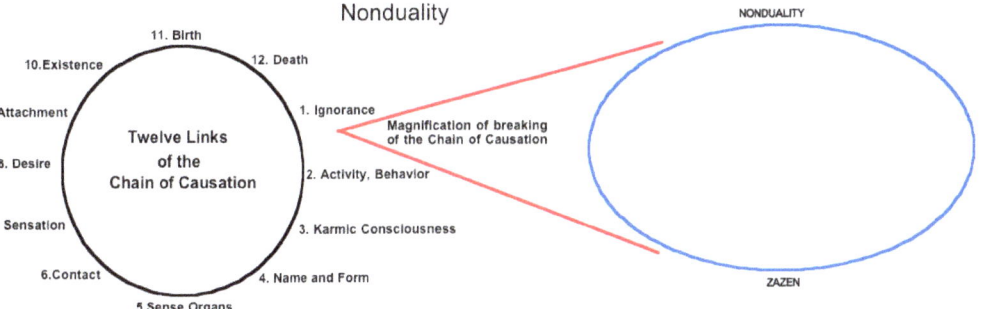

An ellipse is added to the symbol at the furthest extension of the lines of magnification. The enhanced viewpoint drills down to the depths of the relationship between Ignorance and Behavior. Two events are the outcome of taking on the formal practice of Zazen:

- We attain a clearer vision of how conditioned states arise from within Ignorance and affect Behavior.
- The simple act of non-judgmental awareness that is integral to Zazen changes the relationship between Ignorance and Behavior.

The label "Nonduality" on the ellipse indicates that it encompasses the individual's entire personality, action, and experience, while "Zazen" stands for the method and location of the sharpening and focusing of the microscopic eye of meditation. The doubling of the label establishes that the practice of Zazen is the realization of Nonduality. Nonduality excludes nothing. All mental and physical states whether positive or negative are contained within the ellipse.

31

The four meditations taught by Shakyamuni Buddha teach how to gain conceptual understanding of the process of awakening, and then, using that knowledge as a foundation, experience directly the truth of each within meditation practice. The beginning of this practice lies in recognizing our fascination with the familiar. Habits unconsciously mold behavioral responses. To break away from old patterns, practitioners seek the skills to look at the world truthfully, awaken to the possibility of liberation, form an intention to do so, and implement a skillful means to accomplish the goal.

MEDITATION PRACTICED BY BEGINNERS

"Beginners should retire to a quiet and solitary place,
remembering that life-long habits
of discriminative thinking cannot be broken off easily or quickly."[21]
Shakyamuni Buddha in the Lankavatara Sutra

Beginner's meditation refers to the process of emerging from a mental landscape where conditioned states and discriminative thinking unconsciously dominate. An individual begins to become aware of the entrapping actions of conditioned states and the barriers to freedom they cause. A practitioner may experience various kinds of mental and/or physical pain, the sources of which are not clearly understood. After becoming aware of these detrimental influences, one begins to learn how to articulate clear and accurate descriptions of the conditioned states, along with means to resolve them.

At this level, the Universal Mind dawns within the Personal Mind, and the nature of their relationship becomes the central theme of practice. A new perspective and way of living in the world are unveiled, grounded in experiential observation, inquiry, and certainty. Pioneering Zen teachers taught three techniques (among others) for beginners:

- *Mind/Body Relationship*: Experiential awareness of the relationship of physical posture and mental states.
- *The Informal Mind*: The mind becomes relaxed and alert, without limitation or definition. Mental formations within the

mind come and go without preference. However, practitioners establish and cultivate a keen awareness of the life cycles of mental formations, their arising, existence, and dissolution. Mentality is seen as vast, fleeting, and interdependent.

- *Foundation of Practice*: Practitioners articulate their spiritual issue and to begin to comprehend the intimate positive feedback relationship between conditioned states and awakening.

MEDITATION DEVOTED TO THE EXAMINATION OF MEANING

"[The Benefactor] *Sudarshana taught*
the manifestation of the three eyes:
the eye of knowledge that observes faculties,
the objective eye that knows principles,
and the eye of wisdom that understands dualities."
– Flower Ornament Sutra

Using The Three Eyes of Sudarshana provides the knowledge and introspective understanding of the mind's contents and functioning

- *Observes Faculties* means to monitor the functioning of the Five Skandhas, reason, will, cognition, imagination, memory, discrimination, fantasy, creative impulses, etc., and to identify conditioned states, their function, nature and triggers, and their associated afflictive emotions.
- *Knows Principles* establishes understanding the Dharma Seals of Impermanence, Interdependence, and Nirvana (intimacy).
- *Understands Dualities* means to recognize both sides (Personal and Universal) of every internal or external situation, to distinguish their commonalities and differences, and to live within and realize the fundamental harmony of their relationship.

MEDITATION WITH "THUSNESS" FOR ITS OBJECT – *MITSUGO*

"'Mitsu' means 'secret' or 'mystical' in the sense of not apparent to the senses or the intellect, but experienced directly or immediately as if two things are touching. 'Go' means 'words' or 'talk.' So Mitsugo means 'Secret Talk,' that is, something communicated directly without sound. In Buddhism it is said that there is secret talk that can be recognized and understood even though it has no sound. So 'secret talk' suggests the existence of an intuitive perception. It is a fact that we can sometimes discover meaning or secrets without any external stimuli, but we need not see the fact as particularly mystical. An analogy that helps to understand such facts is the sympathetic resonance of tuning forks."[22]

Mitsugo or Secret Talk, has three components:
- The fundamental awareness of the Personal Mind
- The response by the Universal Mind aroused by the stimulus of willful awareness
- The complementary relationship of the Personal and Universal Aspects of Mind that manifests as intuitive perception, otherwise known as Thusness

The intimate interaction of the Personal and Universal aspects of mind introduces the world of Thusness. They beneficially interact, refining the traits and properties of the Personal.

The two attributes of meditation with Thusness for its object are tranquility and insight. Tranquility separates the self from identification with the entities of the mind, allowing insight to arise within consciousness; insight is the product of a mind trained to observe itself, to be aware of its own activities and contents. Tranquility is holding still, embracing the contents of the mind without judgment or preference; insight is accepting the truth of the nonfabricated voice of Thusness. Tung-shan Liang-chieh describes the action of this voice in the *Song of the Jewel Mirror Awareness:*

"Subtly included within the true,
Inquiry and response come up together."

Within the "true," the conscious inquiry of fundamental awareness (the Personal) becomes a liberating force because of its relationship with the meaningful "response" (the Universal). Inquiry and response are not serial events; they are two entangled, secret (*Mitusgo*) activities. The Personal and Universal Aspects of Mind are concordant, inseparable, of equal value, and engaged in intimate and unending relations.

MEDITATION OF THE BUDDHA TATHAGATAS

> *"When the teachings of the Dharma are fully understood*
> *and are perfectly realized by the disciples and masters*
> *that which is realized in their deepest consciousness*
> *is their own Buddha-nature revealed as Tathágata."*[23]
> Shakyamuni Buddha in the Lankavatara Sutra

The meditation of the Buddha Tathágatas is the culmination of the path to Buddhist liberation, where resolving the fundamental misperception and its associated habit energies result in a change in Behavior. Individuals who attain the meditation of the Tathágatas relate to the world fully in both their Personal and Universal aspects, allowing them to live effortlessly and unselfconsciously, freed from previous restrictions.

ARE THE FOUR MEDITATIONS A FORMULA OR NOT?

The Buddha appears to suggest a step-by-step formula for advancing understanding with his teaching of the four stages of meditation, and indeed he is doing just that. The four stages set practitioners on a long journey of increasing awareness of their place in the world. However, the stages are not limited by time nor follow a rigid pattern, but they occur at varying intervals depending on circumstances. The formula exists as a powerful organizational and motivational guideline but without confinement and dogma. The ellipse represents radical nonduality that grants validity to all experience. The four stages offer practitioners freedom of experience within basic instructions. Thus, we have the best of both worlds – the clarity and direction of a well-defined formula acting in harmony with openness.

What is the grammar of awakening for this addition?
The mind of Nonduality – Zazen is all-inclusive and inherently transformative.

Impermanence

"All that can be said, is this, that relatively speaking,
there is a constant stream of becoming,
a momentary and uninterrupted change
from one state of appearance to another."[24]

Shakyamuni Buddha in the Lankavatara Sutra

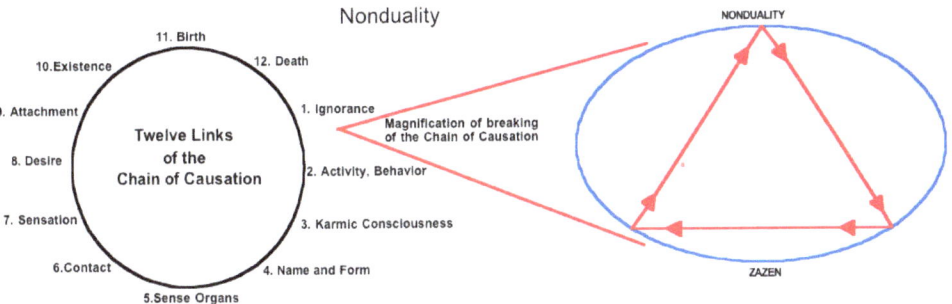

The descriptions of the symbols of the Twelve Links of the Chain of Causation, the Nature of Ignorance, and Zazen and Nonduality express levels of reality that are most often lived unconsciously. Buddhism does not avoid reality; it goes straight for it. The Twelve Links is described as a fact of life; conditioned states are an afflictive reality, and integrity of mind is not a given, but an outcome of study, meditation, and cultivation of insight. Authenticity and wholeness are not ready-made, but a product of choosing the path of mastery of mind. Zazen practice sets in motion the preparation of the ground of awakening.

The increased power of the lines of magnification enables perception of a triangle with arrowheads within the ellipse. This expansive view highlights the interaction of Ignorance and Behavior. The equilateral triangle within the ellipse is the first step of the representation of the three aspects of the process of awakening. The triangle's equal sides symbolize the equal value of each aspect of the process. They were briefly characterized in Chapter 2 as resolving the *dukkha* of conditioned states, refining and integrating the freedom of Thusness, and attaining of unity. In the triangle, the resolution of conditioned states starts on the lower left side followed on subsequent sides by Thusness and unity.

The path pointer arrowheads drawn on the triangle signify impermanence, with the point of the arrow indicating the direction of movement, with placement of two arrowheads on each leg stipulating continuous change. Impermanence is a principle of reality, inevitable for everyone and everything. Our internal and external lives, the natural world around us, and the entire universe changes and unfolds presenting a new pattern each moment in forms that never repeat. Looking at tree on a calm day, the leaves may look the same second to second, but motion is unrelenting, nothing is ever the same, always creating a pristine reality.

Impermanence has two facets brought about by constant change – one that limits and the other that frees. The limitations of impermanence are well-known by all. We experience them hour-by-hour, day-to-day. They require persistent adaptation to unfamiliar situations as they happen. Freedom arises from change as well. On this side individuals mold impermanence for their own benefit. The awareness of Zazen modifies the interaction of Ignorance and Behavior. It is possible to consciously intervene with the automatic process of the Twelve Links, by learning how to resolve conditioned states as they issue from Ignorance. This is the freeing side of Impermanence. It is becoming skilled in the process of awakening and following the path to its culmination.

What is the grammar of awakening for this addition?
Change is inevitable in two ways – an unconscious unfolding of pain, loss, and separation; or choosing to negotiate the path of awareness leading to the cessation of dukkha.

Awakenings

"Error being discriminated by the wise turns into Truth
by virtue of the "turning-about"
that takes place within the deepest consciousness.
Mind, thus emancipated, enters
into perfect self-realization of Noble Wisdom."[25]

Shakyamuni Buddha in the Lankavatara Sutra

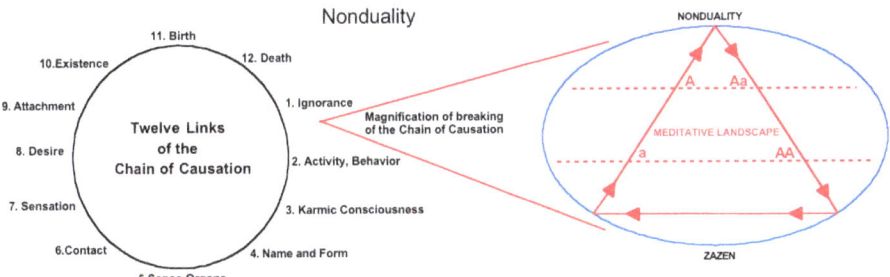

Dashed lines added in the upper and lower areas of the ellipse cut the triangle into three sections. The middle section labeled "Meditative Landscape" indicates the correspondence between the awakenings and Zazen practice. The four points where the lines cross the triangle's sides are marked with 'a' 'A' 'Aa' and 'AA' signifying the time and place where awakenings occur. Awakenings, the "turning-abouts" of the Buddha, are significant life-changing events that are produced by efforts made in the pursuit of awakening. There are two categories of awakenings: perspective and transformative. Perspective awakenings ['a' 'Aa'] modify the orientation of mind, enlarging the conscious view of the self and its constituents. Transformative awakenings ['A' 'AA'] resolve conditioned states and their associated habit energies, bringing about existential changes in being and behavior. The placement of the dashed lines on the triangle shows how the four awakenings relate with the three aspects of the process of awakening; the two awakenings in the first leg resolve conditioned states, and the two others in the second integrate freedom.

Awakenings modify the mental afflictions of conditioned states. These afflictions are the source of intense misery, confounding our best intentions because they are deeply rooted and habitually reveal themselves in negative emotions. Most conditioned states and the mental afflictions that emerge from them can only be resolved with considerable time and directed effort. The awakenings denote the location on the path where conscious efforts yield positive results.

Awakening 'a' is a change of perspective wherein awareness observes a conditioned state as it arises and unfolds. One gains the ability to observe the difference between being unconsciously trapped by a conditioned state and being consciously aware of how it manifests. It is the most difficult awakening to effect for a number of reasons.

- Unfamiliarity with the overall process
- Making the erroneous assumption that Awakening 'a' has already been accomplished when it has not
- Holding the mistaken view that Awakening 'a' is a mere letting go of or cessation of thought
- Not understanding that it takes years to gain the requisite meditative composure and then to learn how to embrace the contents of the conditioned state

Awakening 'A' is a change of being, one that arrives fully formed within consciousness, along with a sense of certainty and joyful rapport. It is an intuitive perception of the liberating force of Thusness, an outcome of an inquiry whose immediate response answers with complete appropriateness the practitioner's engagement with a problem within the process of awakening. The sudden breakthrough to the clarity and freedom of Thusness is not without antecedent struggle. A great deal of time dedicated to prepatory practice on conditioned states precedes the resolution.

Awakening 'Aa' is the ability to observe and begin the integration of the freedom from afflictive emotions and to cultivate the ability to think and feel in entirely new ways brought about by Awakening 'A.' The practitioner's effort centers on how to integrate the freedom into daily life. In Awakening 'a,' a new perspective results from observing the emotional bondage caused by unresolved conditioned states. In Awakening 'Aa' one cultivates another new perspective, that of refining and integrating the freedom of Thusness.

Awakening 'AA' is a change of behavior, the culmination of the path of liberation. The individual who attains Awakening 'AA' relates to the world fully in both its Personal and Universal aspects because the obstructions of the conditioned state are no longer present. Completion of one circle prepares the practitioner for further work on the path identifying and resolving the next conditioned state. As the path pointer arrowheads suggest, numerous trips around the triangle are necessary.

What is the grammar of awakening for this addition?
Awakenings are the pathways of freedom.

The Three Aspects of the Process of Awakening

"The Bodhisattva …walks the path leading to Nirvana.
Thereon his mind will unfold by perceiving, thinking,
meditating, and abiding in the practice of
concentration until he attains the "turning-about" at
the source of habit-energy;
he will thereafter lead a life of excellent deeds."[26]
Shakyamuni Buddha in the Lankavatara Sutra

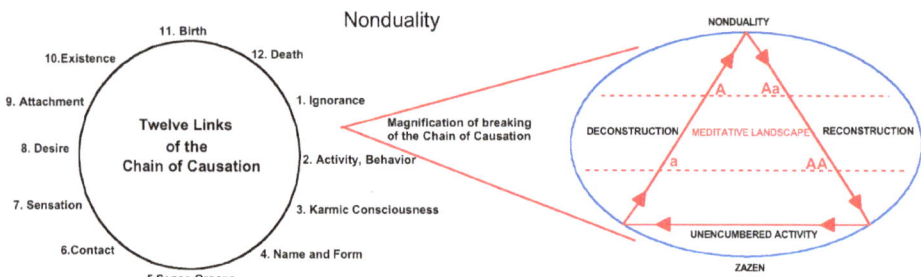

The three aspects of the process of awakening include resolving the *dukkha* of conditioned states (Deconstruction, intuitive perception), refining and integrating the freedom of Thusness (Reconstruction, transformation), and attainment of unity (Unencumbered Activity, Noble Wisdom).

Three terms, Deconstruction, Reconstruction, and Unencumbered Activity, appear on the symbol. With the additions, the symbol now possesses all the elements of Zen Buddhist instruction to understand the nature of Ignorance and to sever the Twelve Links. The terms Deconstruction, Reconstruction, and Unencumbered Activity are not Buddhist in origin, but represent Buddhist teachings on the three aspects of the process of awakening. They were chosen to keep the symbol as clear as possible of the usual technical terms. Later chapters will bring the new and customary expressions together. For now, we will proceed with the assigned designations.

Conditioned states arise from within Ignorance and immediately begin to shape Behavior. The awareness gained through Zazen builds up a detailed understanding of their forms and function over time. However, conditioned states are difficult to perceive initially, requiring directed effort. The processes of Deconstruction, Reconstruction, and Unencumbered Activity contain the means to engage creatively with habituated forms of consciousness, ultimately leading to liberation from their tyranny.

Deconstruction and Reconstruction define the four dispositions of conditioning that require attention in order to transform consciousness. The four are:

In Deconstruction

- The harmful effects of conditioned states are internalized. Negative emotions associated with conditioned states are allowed to be what they are internally, but not expressed outwardly.
- Uprooting of conditioned states at their source in Ignorance

In Reconstruction

- Integrates the freedom of Thusness by working with habit energies left over from the resolution of conditioned states
- Overcomes the vestiges of the conditioned states granting the ability to live freely

The four dispositions roughly correspond to the four awakenings. In Deconstruction, the observational perspective of Awakening 'a' furnishes the ability to separate from the grip of the conditioned states and the tendency to project their afflictive affects. Not projecting negative emotions generates creative tension that ultimately serves the process of their resolution. The intuitive perception of Awakening 'A' overturns the psychophysical formations associated with a conditioned state that was previously taken as the authentic.

The process of Deconstruction consciously engages with conditioned states that are rooted in negative learning stored as psychophysical formations. This effort, if taken through to completion, ultimately resolves these formations, freeing one from the suffering that arises from them. The process of Deconstruction moves from conditioning toward freedom. It brings about greater awareness of the complementary interplay between the Personal and Universal foci of wholeness, offering a means to eliminate the barriers caused by conditioned states that impede the full freedom of that interplay.

In Reconstruction, Awakening 'Aa' incorporates the insight of Thusness gained in Awakening 'A' into daily life while working on dissipating the lingering habit energies. Awakening 'AA' produces a transformative change of behavior making responses to life natural and in accord with the needs of oneself and others.

Reconstruction is concerned with integrating freedom and eliminating the remaining habit energies of the uprooted conditioned state. Reconstruction is learning to live the freedom realized in Awakening 'A.' The entire process of Reconstruction can be considered a conscious cultivation and integration of the vision and freedom of Awakening 'A.' Reconstruction deals with liberation – the unimpeded activity of the Personal and Universal aspects of being.

The bottom line of the triangle is Unencumbered Activity symbolizing Nonduality in action, resulting from completion of Reconstruction. The conscious work of Deconstruction and Reconstruction liberates the self from the imprisoning effects of conditioned states evoking "a life of excellent deeds."

What is the grammar of awakening for this addition?
The Zen dialogue demonstrates the intimate interplay of the Personal and Universal Aspects of Mind.

SUMMARY
The six symbols of the first magnification validate Buddhism as a teaching of actuality and relationships. They map an increasing experiential penetration from the startling and hard-won realization of the nature of the Twelve Links of the Chain of Causation, through to a holistic view of the process of awakening, where awakening represents the intimate interconnection of the "parts" of the universe.

The Dōgen scholar Hee-Jin Kim terms this penetration the "existential metabolism of nonduality."

Each symbol grows out of a cluster of basic teachings, generating a refined understanding in its grammar of awakening. The symbol illustrates wholeness, duality, the three aspects of awakening, the four awakenings, impermanence, Alaya consciousness, and other teachings to ground their veracity and to show how they bond and interrelate. The outcome is a common understanding effective for individual study and group communication. The Nonduality Symbol clarifies gathered information and its importance, and tracks the progress of awakening within an individual's life.

Chapter 4
Second Magnification
The Nonduality – Resolution Sequence Symbol

"The illusions of the mind and the infatuations of egoism,
such things as fear, anger, hatred and pride;
these are purified by study and meditation" [27]

Shakyamuni Buddha in the Lankavatara Sutra

The Symbol of Nonduality generated in the first magnification resulted from a level of enhancement analogous to the improvement in vision an optical lens microscope furnishes compared to ordinary sight. The Dutch opticians who devised the original microscopes in the seventeenth century saw "little animals" wriggling around – the first view of cellular life. Subsequent improvements such as compounding the lenses and grinding them for color correction, in time, brought the optical microscope to its present level of capability. The electron scanning microscope that scans with an electron beam rather than light, outperforms the optical units by two thousand times, allowing objects as small as atoms to be seen. The second magnification, the Nonduality – Resolution Sequence Symbol, employs a similar degree of increased vision as the electronic microscope in comparison to the optical. This means a whole new gradation of insight uncovers the "atomic" detail of the process of awakening.

The Symbol of Nonduality itself includes all the elements necessary to commence and negotiate the way of Buddha. However, to our benefit, the symbolic method promotes and inspires imaginative approaches to new thinking. In this case, completing the six symbols of the first magnification opened the way for the second magnification provided by the Resolution Sequence. The triggers, forms, and functions of the conditioned states come into view provided because of this greatly expanded perspective. The improved outlook facilitates a finer understanding of the inner workings that occur before, during, and after life-altering awakenings.

The inspiration derived from the Symbol of Nonduality exhibits the open-ended possibilities and the powers of symbols to push through barriers and create new combinations of the traditional and new. The Nonduality – Resolution Sequence Symbol brings together the ancient teaching of Zen and the psychotherapy of David Grove. Both streams of learning and healing are information-based teachings that acknowledge and respect the wisdom that arises from the Universal Mind, though Grove never defined his method that way. In both cases, the sought-for information results from appropriate methods of inquiry formed internally or received from the outside. This combination of Buddhism and science is an example that comes about from their mutual interest. Both hard and soft fields of science already find significant concurrence with Buddhist thought as both emphasize non-metaphysical explorations of reality and relationships. Buddhism will be a willing and able partner with science's burgeoning need and desire to incorporate the study of consciousness within its range of interest.

The second magnification adds the Resolution Sequence stage labels to Deconstruction and Reconstruction to define the inner workings that occur during the process of awakening. This may seem at odds with the symbol versus rhetoric argument made in Chapter 1. As we shall see, the labels are transitional devices created to foster ways that deepen the connection between conceptual and experiential understanding.

Nonduality – Resolution Sequence
and
Zazen – Introspection

"[Buddha] discovered the form of meditation leading to
the complete liberation of mind, to the realization of Nirvana....
This is essentially Buddhist meditation, Buddhist mental culture.
It is an analytical method based on mindfulness, awareness, vigilance, and observation."[28]
Walpola Rahula in *What the Buddha Taught*

The Elements of the Resolution Sequence - 1

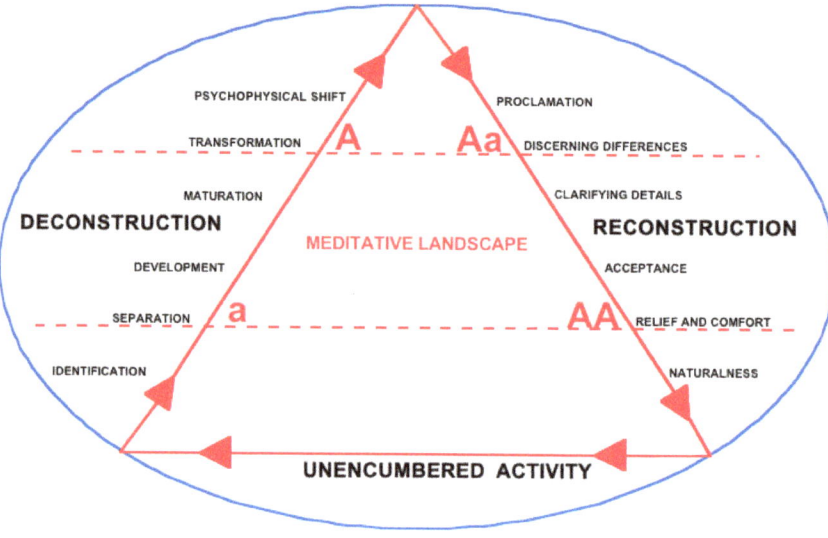

We begin the second magnification with a copy of the Three Aspects of the Process Awakening Symbol, the final version of the first magnification, without picturing the Twelve Links. The links are still active, just not shown. Twelve labels describing the process of awakening illustrate the stages of Deconstruction and Reconstruction. Also, now in place, are the modified symbol titles of Nonduality –

Resolution Sequence which refers to the twelve labels, and Zazen – Introspection which points out the increased emphasis of Zazen practice in working with the content of conditioned states. The process of awakening illustrated by the Nonduality – Resolution Sequence Symbol contains both the classic elements of Zen practice and the introspective method of the Resolution Sequence.

The twelve stages of Deconstruction and Reconstruction are guides to an experiential understanding of the unfolding of awakening. Each of the stages performs two services:

- To summarize the action and results of the process of awakening at the juncture where each stage operates

- To supply direction for correct orientation.

The Resolution Sequence puts into words an introspective method that instructs practitioners in working with conditioned states. *Introspective analysis into the operation and resolution of conditioned states naturalizes the inner dialogue between the Personal and Universal Aspects of Mind.* Observation and questioning continue their definitive roles as the chief means of gathering experiential evidence. Acquiring conscious knowledge of conditioned states provides the basis for understanding the best methods for practice to avoid wasteful efforts.

The table below lists the twelve symbol labels and a one-word definition for each of them. Practitioners can memorize the table and refer to the stages' labels to navigate the persistently changing needs of the process. Brief interpretations of each stage are also included.

Deconstruction	Reconstruction
1. Identification – *Articulating*	7. Proclamation – *Asserting*
2. 'a' Separation – *Observing*	8. **'Aa'** Discerning Differences – *Noting*
3. Development – *Questioning*	9. Clarifying Details – *Opening*
4. Maturation – *Embracing*	10. Acceptance – *Having*
5. **'A'** Transformation – *Liberating*	11. **'AA'** Relief and Comfort – *Being*
6. Psychophysical Shift – *Shedding*	12. Naturalness – *Sharing*

Deconstruction

1. Identification – *Articulating*

   Identification has two aspects: the absence of questioning, and the beginning of understanding the nature of repetitive mental affliction. Without reflection and inquiry, the unfolding life just happens within a single perspective, defined by whatever momentary perception is occurring. *Articulating* means gaining the ability to name the conditioned state that is active at any given moment.

2. Awakening '**a**' Separation – *Observing*

   An observational viewpoint is gained through Zen training. In Zazen, one acquires the ability to witness conditioned states and inquire into their function. *Observing* discerns the difference between being unconsciously trapped by a conditioned state and being consciously aware of how it manifests.

3. Development – *Questioning*

   Development is where conditioned states begin to deconstruct. *Questioning* cultivates the awareness of the connections between negative emotions, mental pain, and conditioned states.

4. Maturation – *Embracing*

   Maturation provides the practitioner with the inner firmness and strength required to recognize, accept, and keep the effects of conditioned states internalized. *Embracing* minimizes projection of negative responses into the world. Not projecting negative emotions generates creative tension that ultimately serves the process of their resolution. In Maturation, daily life reflects the creative interplay of the complementary pair of mental afflictions and awakening.

5. Awakening 'A' Transformation – *Liberating*

   The conditioned state and its related afflictive pain are resolved. The pain changes from a symptomatic issue to productive energy and insight. *Liberating* means transformation of the conditioned state and resolution of the associated afflictive emotions. Liberating moves the practitioner beyond coping.

6. Psychophysical Shift – *Shedding*

The Psychophysical Shift unburdens the practitioner of the mental habits and deep-seated assumptions embedded in the conditioned state. An individual's experience of self is radically altered without the conditioned state's encumbrance. *Shedding* establishes an entirely new point of reference that replaces one that was formally taken as normal, predictable, and essential. One is relieved of the negative psychophysical effects of the conditioned state. Transformation and Psychophysical Shift modify one's inner ecology.

Reconstruction

7. Proclamation – *Asserting*

Proclamation captures the content of the moment: the change issued through Transformation announces that the old way of being has passed, and a new spiritual dimension now animates the core of one's efforts. Freedom from the pain of afflictive emotions becomes the norm. *Asserting* forcefully acknowledges the changeover from concentration on a conditioned state to living the truth of freedom.

8. Awakening **'Aa'** Discerning Differences – *Noting*

Practitioners examine the connection between a psychophysical shift and freedom from afflictive pain. When the physical or mental remnants of the conditioned state appear, they are experienced as rootless and ephemeral. *Noting* witnesses that habitual patterns associated with conditioned states no longer have the power to cause afflictive responses.

9. Clarifying Details – *Opening*

In Clarifying Details, the practitioner clearly articulates observed differences, appreciating and enjoying them as freedom, while drawing upon them for reflection. *Opening* means not being trapped by a premature sense of satisfaction thinking everything is all right.

10. Acceptance – *Having*

Acceptance grounds the practitioner's trust and confidence in the durability of the changes experienced during Reconstruction. *Having* fully grasps the significance of the transition from the problematic symptom, but effort is still required to recognize habit energies.

11. Awakening **'AA'** Relief and Comfort – *Being*

Relief and Comfort culminates in the attainment of unity. *Being* means a breakthrough to a change of behavior. Habit energies connected with the resolved conditioned state no longer arise.

12. Naturalness – *Sharing*

Naturalness is activated awareness, with Unencumbered Activity the effortless outcome. *Sharing* means the Personal and Universal Aspects of Mind respond to the demands of changing circumstances with authenticity.

While Zazen practice provides the intuition to uncover the composition of conditioned states, the Resolution Sequence advances understanding of that knowledge. During Deconstruction one systematically acknowledges and clarifies the barriers to Transformation. Reconstruction is concerned with integrating the freedom experienced in Transformation and eliminating habit energies.

The Nonduality – Resolution Sequence Symbol's composition includes all the tools to identify conditioned states, limit their harmful effects, transform them into avenues of freedom, and ultimately put an end to habit energies. One can use the symbol just as it is and enjoy significant results. However, practitioners conversant in its application can internalize the process so that a minimum of conscious reflection is required when in use, speeding the process. The next five symbols document the internalizing of the Nonduality – Resolution Sequence Symbol. Each version of the symbol shows a significant step of deepening understanding.

What is the grammar of awakening for this addition?
The Resolution Sequence offers knowledge and direction essential for awakening.

Gradual and Sudden Awakenings

"The purification of the [conditioning] *of mind
is at best slow and gradual, requiring both zeal and patience.
But ... the self-realization of Noble Wisdom is a purification
that comes instantaneously by the grace of the Tathágatas."*[29]
Shakyamuni Buddha in the Lankavatara Sutra

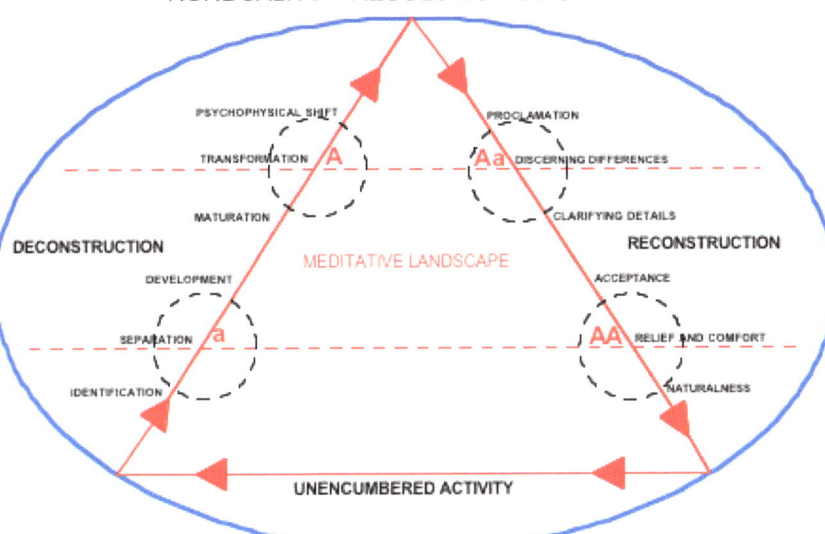

The Elements of the Resolution Sequence - 2
NONDUALITY – RESOLUTION SEQUENCE

PSYCHOPHYSICAL SHIFT

TRANSFORMATION A   Aa DISCERNING DIFFERENCES

MATURATION   CLARIFYING DETAILS

DECONSTRUCTION   RECONSTRUCTION

MEDITATIVE LANDSCAPE

DEVELOPMENT   ACCEPTANCE

SEPARATION a   AA RELIEF AND COMFORT

IDENTIFICATION   NATURALNESS

UNENCUMBERED ACTIVITY

PROCLAMATION

ZAZEN – INTROSPECTION

The French mathematician, Henri Poincaré, described his mathematical efforts as "conscious introspection followed by inspiration," which also happens to be an apt depiction of the essential efforts to facilitate awakenings when engaging with the stages of the Resolution Sequence.

In the Gradual and Sudden Awakenings Symbol, the small dashed-line circles surrounding the four awakenings express the awakenings' heightened importance. The awakenings spread out and integrate the stages before and after. Practitioners pay less attention to achieving awakenings as they secure experience with the Resolution Sequence,. They scrutinize more closely the afflictive emotions within the stages of Deconstruction, because they know the quickest path to awakening lies at the heart of the conditioned state and its associated negativity. The same is true of the stages of Reconstruction except awareness focuses on penetrating the nature and activity of the freedom of Awakening 'A.' Each of the awakenings occupies a critical setting within the Resolution Sequence.

Awakening 'a' Identification – Separation – Development

Awakening 'a' is a change of perspective produced within Zazen practice that transforms one's worldview from "mundane only" to witnessing the sacred. Awakening 'a' is the gradual understanding of the reality of conditioned states and how they produce afflictive emotions. The effort to awaken is aroused only when awareness of the Universal Mind has strength and power; awareness of the truth of the Twelve Links of the Chain of Causation and how it functions provides that power. In the stage of Identification, a growing awareness of one's existential predicament motivates the practice of Zazen that unveils the Universal Mind. Attaining Separation means accepting the Universal Mind as real. This is a world-view changing event, simultaneously providing an observational space between oneself, conditioned states, and their reactive emotional responses.

Awakening 'A' Maturation – Transformation – Psychophysical Shift

In Maturation, impartiality embraces the conditioned state establishing the creative tension that is the motivating force of Transformation. Awakening 'A' launches practitioners into a new world where the stranglehold of the conditioned state is suddenly and permanently uprooted, unburdening them of the mental habits and deep-seated assumptions embedded in the conditioned state. Such breakthroughs generally are sudden events. Feelings of release, openness, and relaxation replace physical and mental constraints. The Universal Mind comes compellingly to the forefront, and one experiences a change of being.

Awakening 'Aa' Proclamation – Discerning Differences – Clarifying Details

The habit energies of an entrenched conditioned state do not completely dissolve at Transformation. Awakening 'Aa' is a new perspective that step-by-step discerns the differences between freedom and affliction. When the physical or mental remnants of the conditioned state appear, they are experienced as rootless and ephemeral. These habitual patterns associated with the conditioned states no longer cause afflictive responses. The vestigial habit energies draw attention but without influence or control. The Universal and Personal Minds beneficially interact, refining the attributes of the Personal.

Awakening 'AA' Acceptance – Relief and Comfort – Naturalness

Awakening 'AA' is a change of behavior. Habit energies dissipate. The Personal and Universal attain unity acting as complements with unobstructed harmony. It is the Middle Way of Buddhism, where the Personal (the mind of discrimination) and Universal (the mind of unity) manifest with equal importance.

What is the grammar of awakening for this addition?
The sudden and gradual awakenings are inseparable and act as complements.

The Everyday Mind

"The residue of the resolved conditioned state is more easily dealt with. Now only minimal effort is required to dismiss the rootless and powerless tendencies connected with it."[30]

The Elements of the Resolution Sequence - 3

NONDUALITY – RESOLUTION SEQUENCE

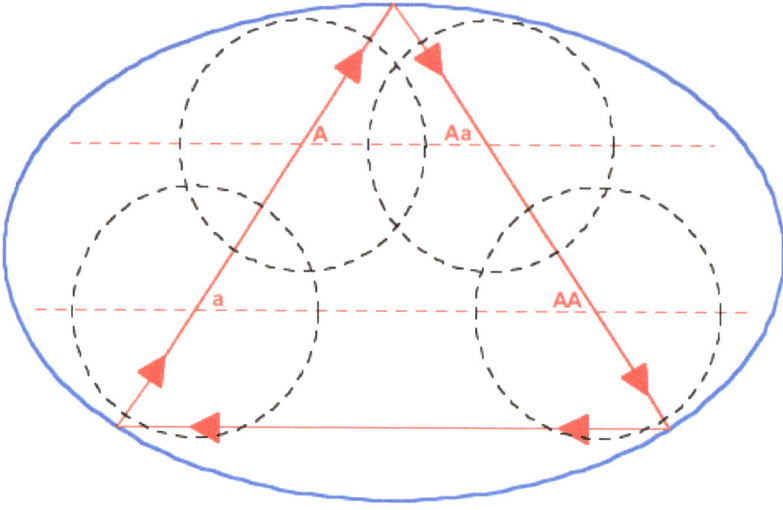

ZAZEN – INTROSPECTION

The dashed circles centered on the four awakenings expand and displace all of the Resolution Sequence labels. Even though the labels are gone, the mind of the practitioner considers and takes action inspired by their wisdom. The awakenings occur with the same ease and consonance as a master violinist performing a concerto. The awakenings and music flow from the same source.

The overlapping circles indicate rapid internal insights and transformations. Conditioned states' speed of resolution is in lock step with the depth of the process of internalization. It is similar to the unspoken directions that an internal knowledge of the grammar of algebra provides. The hesitancy of inexperience gradually morphs into a familiarity that, in turn, becomes mastery of mind, from which intuitive perceptions appear with the same ease as echoes arrive from an original sound.

What is the grammar of awakening for this addition?
The Personal and Universal Aspects of Mind relate in harmonious interplay.

Trust and Confidence

"Mahamati, you, and all Bodhisattvas
should discipline yourselves in the realization
and patient acceptance of the truths of emptiness, …
and the Nonduality of all things."[31]

Shakyamuni Buddha in the Lankavatara Sutra

The Elements of the Resolution Sequence - 4

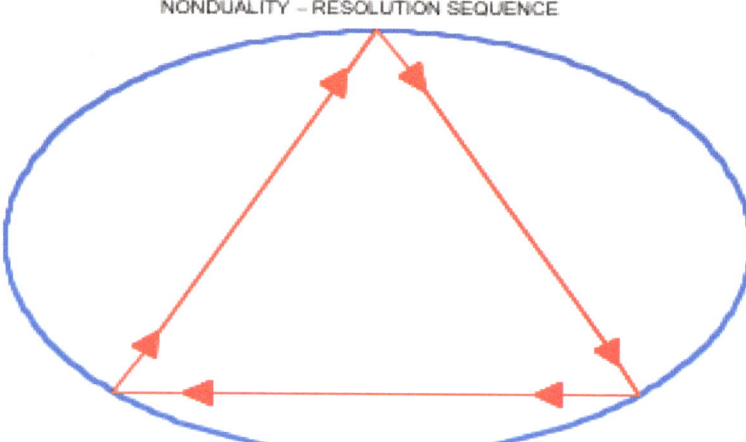

NONDUALITY – RESOLUTION SEQUENCE

ZAZEN – INTROSPECTION

Trust and confidence are the indispensable components of Buddhist faith. With trust, the intuitive understanding welling up from the depths of the Universal Mind informs daily life with confidence. This symbol retains the three sides of practice and impermanence, discarding all labels. The need for illustration lessens, as the practice gradually becomes second nature. Liberation manifests in the validity and durability of the changes experienced. One can fully grasp the significance of the transition from the problematic symptom to Buddhist freedom.

In her book *Luminous Emptiness*, Francesca Fremantle succinctly defines the difference between Buddhist and other spiritual teachings. "[In Buddhism] *liberation is not of the self, but from the self.*"[32] "Liberation of the self" presupposes that if one tries hard enough on the road of self-improvement, one will find freedom from suffering. Instead, Buddha taught that our understanding of the self that is the problem, and no amount of self-improvement leads to liberation. Liberation of the self is the "normal" viewpoint from which most human activity proceeds. First, we imagine ourselves to harbor some imperfection. Then we make plans to overcome the imperfection. Trying to improve oneself is a worthy pursuit that leads to many benefits for individuals, as well as society at large. This way enhances development of comfort, convenience, safety, and it also ameliorates social issues. However, along this path there is no absolute that ensures final contentment. There is no end to desires that are possible candidates for attention.

In liberation from the self, the goal is not perfection; the objective is freedom from the tyranny of self. Liberation from the self allows us to recognize how much conditioned states impinge on our everyday existence. Mastery of Zazen – Introspection frees the practitioner from the oppression of conditioned states.

What is the grammar of awakening for this addition?
Liberation is possible.

Change of Behavior

"While having relations with an objective world,
there is no rising in the minds of the Tathágatas
of discriminations between the interests of self
and the interests of others, between good and evil, there is
just the spontaneity and effortless actuality of perfect behavior."[33]
Shakyamuni Buddha in the Lankavatara Sutra

The Elements of the Resolution Sequence - 5

NONDUALITY – RESOLUTION SEQUENCE

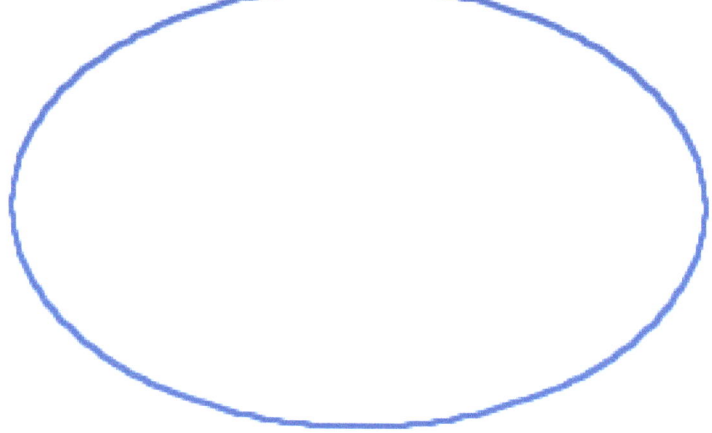

ZAZEN – INTROSPECTION

All that is left is an ellipse, a slightly disfigured circle. An ellipse has two focus points, a circle just one. This   symbol is an ellipse rather than a circle because the foci are not yet in total harmony. The focus points remain a short distance apart, with little in their way to influence adversely their union. The ellipse of the Change of Behavior Symbol is radically different from the ellipse of Zazen and Nonduality of the first magnification. Both ellipses are all-inclusive, but what they include is wildly divergent. The first ellipse signified an out of control Twelve Lnks of the Chain of Causation, with little awareness and insight to countermand the ceaseless eruptions of conditioned states. The Change of Behavior ellipse represents a close complementary relationship of the Personal and Universal Aspects of Mind, the product of freedom that resolving conditioned states brings about.

Buddhism is essentially a teaching of relationships. It promotes a pragmatic approach. Hindrances, such as negative emotions, give way to happy and mutually beneficial social interactions. An abiding sense of accomplishment replaces mental obscurations. Practitioners gain the capability to recognize, accept, and take pleasure in the joy of freedom. The dualistic pair of the Personal and Universal Aspects of Mind is seen to be, and always has been, a creative complement; it is the wisdom that realizes the conventional and ultimate minds are inseparable, of equal value, and engaged in immediate and unending relations.

What is the grammar of awakening for this addition?
One thought of harmony is a moment of Buddhahood.

Naturalness

"The Teaching leads into the real universe,
to merge with the complete embodiment of the fundamental root,
and arrive at the realm of the great knowledge of the real universe
that originally underlies unawareness,
thus, naturally to be rewarded with boundless virtue."
— Flower Ornament Sutra

The Elements of the Resolution Sequence - 6
NONDUALITY – RESOLUTION SEQUENCE

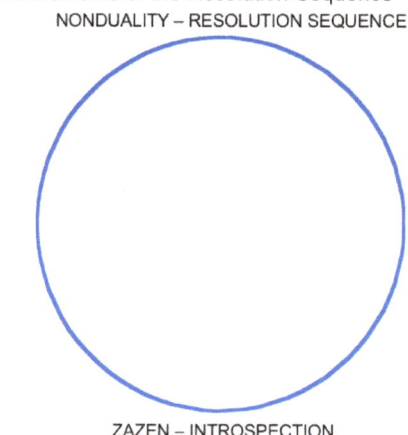

ZAZEN – INTROSPECTION

Impulses of wisdom and caring arise continuously, bestowed like a gift. The *Brahma Viharas* of kindness, compassion, nonspecific gratitude, and intimacy express themselves effortlessly in small and grand ways. Unencumbered Activity prepares one for another trip around the Resolution Sequence to continue the perpetual practice of resolution of conditioned states.

What is the grammar of awakening for this addition?
In naturalness, one is truly ordinary.

SUMMARY

The second magnification introduced the Resolution Sequence and the depth of introspection that comes with its practice. The

Resolution Sequence speeds up the process of integration of the benefits of awakenings and management of habit energies. When the Resolution Sequence becomes second nature, an experienced practitioner can use it to generate additional symbols. This magnification produced six more levels of basic teachings and additional items of grammar of awakening.

Chapter 5
Symbols and the
Grammar of Awakening

"Individual symbols may not have much effect
on a mathematician's creative thinking,
but in groups they acquire powerful connections through
similarity, association, identity, resemblance, and repeated imagery.
They may even create thoughts that are below awareness."[34]
Joseph Mazur in *Enlightening Symbols*

The symbols of Chapters 3 and 4 present in graphical form what occurs at the first two links of the Twelve Links of the Chain of Causation. The symbols elucidate what is not seen by ordinary vision. With the microscopic eye of Zazen, one observes deep aspects of the first two links' relationship, and what becomes visible in the magnified vision is assigned an emblematic meaning and positioned in the symbol. Equally important, this same act of awareness initiates and continues to break the Twelve Links automatic progression, proclaiming the importance of the efforts of the process of awakening. Fundamental awareness does not need to seek to break the chain; breaking the chain is integral to the nature of awareness.

In Chapter 1, questions were posed whether symbols could be an effective skillful means in facilitating awakening in Zen practice. It would be premature to try answering those questions now. That assessment is best left to the summary chapter. However, we can review the results of the symbolization of essential Buddhist concepts and the grammar of awakening that arose from each new image. Also, we will review Buddha's teachings on the intuitive mind, and how they relate to the Nonduality – Resolution Sequence Symbol.

BUDDHIST CONCEPTS
The Nonduality – Resolution Sequence Symbol embraces several major Buddhist tenets, including the teachings underlying

Nonduality, dualistic thought, the three aspects of the process of awakening, and the four awakenings.

Nonduality

The expansion lines unveil the ellipse and the Nonduality (wholeness) of being. All activities within the bounds of the ellipse are constituents of the nondual mind. At this time, the wholeness is one of fragmented emotional and mental chaos. For example, one beginner commented on the state of her mentality, "Will you look what's going on here?" Turning inward just for moment revealed for her how far the actuality of her mind differed from what she formerly conceived it to be. Viewing the all-inclusive ellipse's contents and action reveals it to be filled with out of control-mental-activity.

Dualistic Thought

The ellipse contains the myriad dualities of our makeup and their cumulative actions illustrating two important points:

- The two foci required to draw an ellipse represent the two sides of dualistic thinking. They are complementary components of Nonduality.
- The mind of Nonduality does not transcend dualistic thinking. Rather Nonduality is the complementary sum of duality.

The Three Aspects of the Process of Awakening

Deconstruction, Reconstruction, and Unencumbered Activity are the three aspects of the process of awakening, the three sides of the equilateral triangle. In orthodox Buddhist terminology they are the triple body of Buddha consisting of the activity-body of the Nirmanakaya, the perfect reward-body of Sambhogakaya Buddha, and the reality-body of Dharmakaya. The activity-body of Nirmanakaya consciously pursues transformations where conditioned states are encountered, embraced, and resolved. The perfect reward-body of Sambhogakaya reveals Thusness (*Tathata*) and the path to freedom from the remaining habit energies. The reality-body of Dharmakaya transcends knowledge, manifesting as an intimate intuitive relationship with the Tathágatas, where wisdom and compassion arise from the unified activity of the Personal and Universal Aspects of Mind.

Four Awakenings

The four awakenings occur where the lines marking the boundaries of the Meditative Landscape intersect the triangle sides. They are transition points that mark changes within conditioned states. There are two awakenings each in Deconstruction and Reconstruction. The two in Deconstruction identify and resolve conditioned states; the second two in Reconstruction integrate and refine the freedom of resolution, displacing habit energies leftover from the resolved conditioned state. Placement of the transition points defines their relationship to the Meditative Landscape and the elements of the Resolution Sequence. The conditioned states transform with conscious effort. In concert with the transformations, in small and large ways, practitioners free themselves from the conditioned states' adverse effects. The arrowhead pointers illustrate the necessity of continuous conscious efforts.

The twelve stages of the Resolution Sequence encompass the four awakenings. Each awakening centers on a Resolution Sequence stage, preceded by a preparatory stage and followed by another stage that validates the awakening. The relationship usually unwinds slowly, but that might not be the case in the real world. The time from first stage to last could be fifteen minutes or fifteen years.

GRAMMAR OF AWAKENING

The statements of the grammar of awakening summarize the most salient point of each symbol. They are analogous to the unspoken guidelines that direct problem solving of algebraic equations. In algebra, grammar tells the mathematician when and how to perform a calculation. In our system, for studying the sequence of transformation in Buddhist practice, the statements of grammar are foundational meanings underlying the symbols. For example, study and meditating on the Twelve Links confirm its nature. What the Twelve Links are, and how they function, becomes recognized as an experiential fact of existence. That conclusion is a tacit ingredient of continuing analysis. All other statements of grammar of awakening act in the same way, expressing the actuality of experience in a short sentence of what the symbols intend to convey.

The statements of the grammar of awakening speak for themselves. However, grouping them together with their associated symbols invites greater familiarity, offering an opportunity to witness unrecognized connections. Grouping also shows the organized growth of the process of awakening in the changing symbols, and makes them easier to memorize. The intimate linking of symbol and grammar brings about the desired effect of a wide nuance of meaning, establishing a spacious mental environment. Like the symbologies of mathematics and language, the symbols of awakening when they become second nature, impart the same sureness of comprehension and expression.

FIRST MAGNIFICATION SYMBOLS

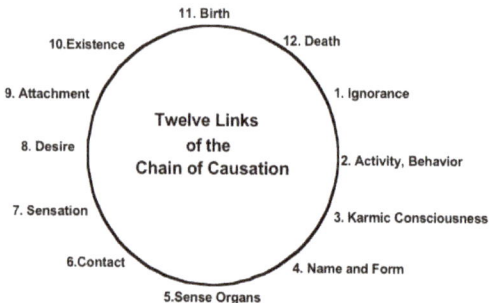

Twelve Links in the Chain of Causation

The Twelve Links of the Chain of Causation is recognized as a fact of existence.

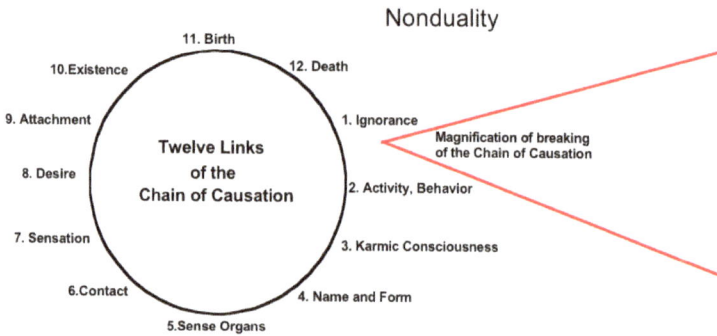

Understanding the Nature of Ignorance

The lines of magnification reveal the experiential reality of conditioned states.

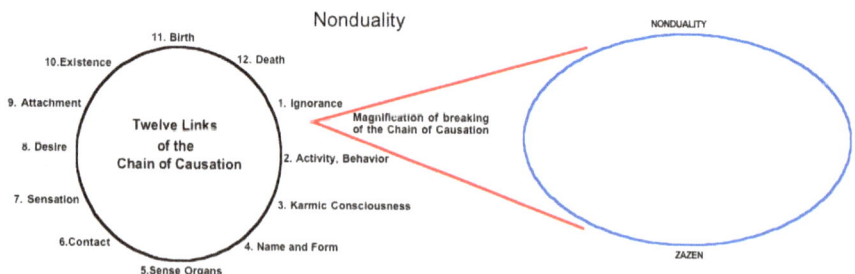

Zazen and Nonduality

The mind of Nonduality – Zazen is all-inclusive and inherently transformative.

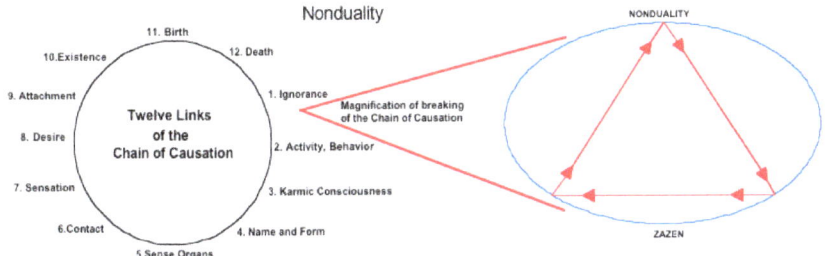

Impermanence

Change is inevitable in two ways – an unconscious unfolding of pain, loss, and separation; or choosing to negotiate the path of awareness leading to the cessation of dukkha.

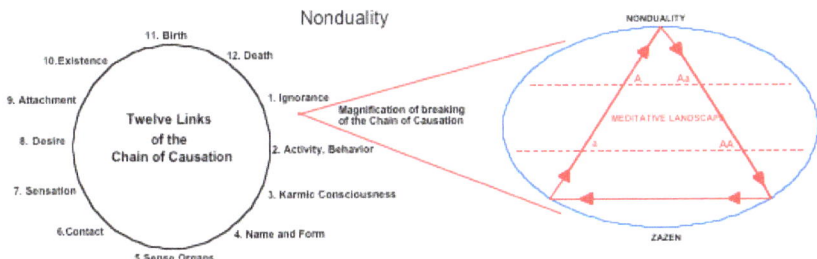

Awakenings

Awakenings are the pathways of freedom.

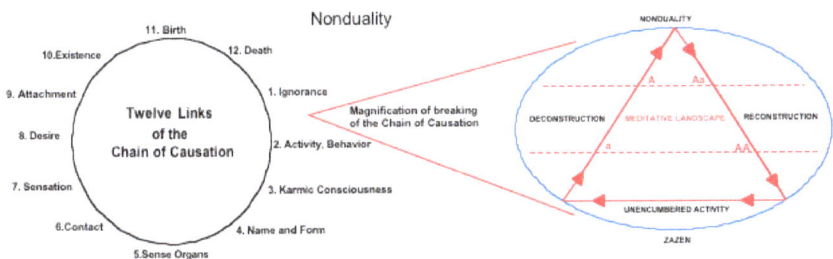

The Three Aspects of the Process of Awakening

The Zen dialogue demonstrates the intimate interplay of the Personal and Universal Aspects of Mind.

SECOND MAGNIFICATION SYMBOLS

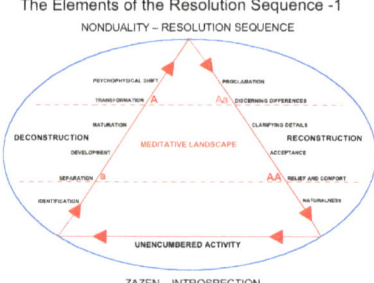

Nonduality – Resolution Sequence   Zazen – Introspection

The Resolution Sequence offers the knowledge and direction essential for awakening.

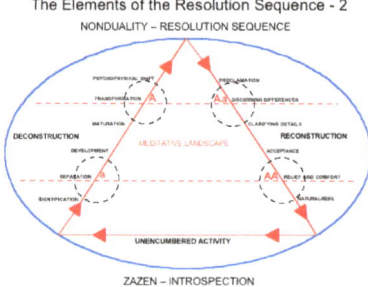

Gradual and Sudden Awakenings

The sudden and gradual awakenings are inseparable and act as complements

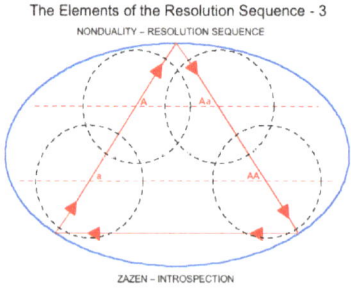

The Everyday Mind

The Personal and Universal Aspects of Mind relate in harmonious interplay

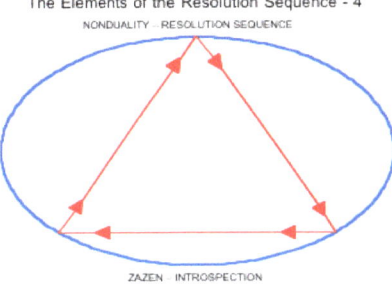

The Elements of the Resolution Sequence - 4

NONDUALITY · RESOLUTION SEQUENCE

ZAZEN · INTROSPECTION

Trust and confidence
Liberation is possible.

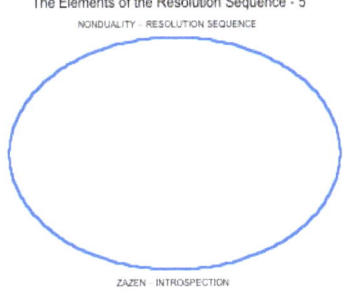

The Elements of the Resolution Sequence - 5

NONDUALITY · RESOLUTION SEQUENCE

ZAZEN · INTROSPECTION

Change of Behavior
One thought of harmony is a moment of Buddhahood.

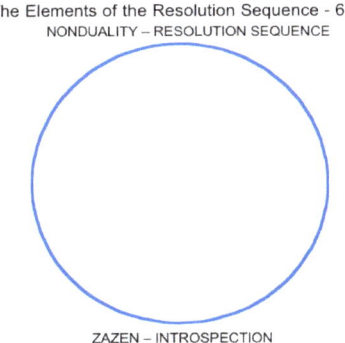

The Elements of the Resolution Sequence - 6

NONDUALITY – RESOLUTION SEQUENCE

ZAZEN – INTROSPECTION

Naturalness
In naturalness, one is truly ordinary.

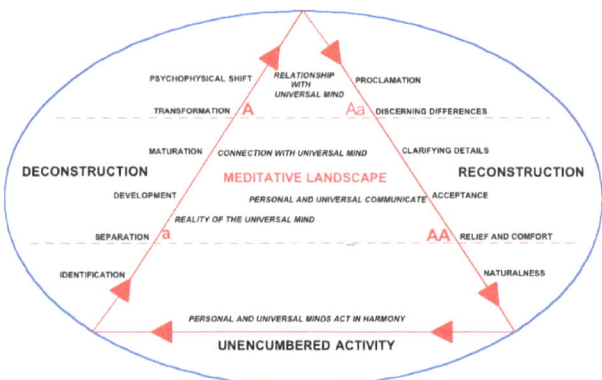

Buddha's Teaching of the Personal and Universal Minds
NONDUALITY – RESOLUTION SEQUENCE

ZAZEN – INTROSPECTION

THE FACULTY OF INTUITION

In the opening quotation from the Lankavatara Sutra in Chapter 3, Shakyamuni Buddha taught that the intuitive mind, also known as the faculty of intuition, arises from the purity of the Universal Mind and acts as the mediator between the Personal and Universal Aspects of Mind. The five statements below summarize how the relationship of the Personal and Universal Aspects of Mind matures from a beginner's first acknowledgement of the Universal, developing into a dialogue of unobstructed harmony.

- Recognizing the reality of the Universal Mind
- Establishing an intuitive engagement with the Universal Mind
- Attaining an open and intimate relationship with the Universal Mind
- The Personal and Universal Aspects of Mind intimately communicate
- The Personal and Universal Aspects of Mind act in unobstructed harmony

Combining the statements on intuition and the Nonduality – Resolution Sequence Symbol shows how they fit together with the stages of the Resolution Sequence. For example, *Recognizing the reality of the Universal Mind* occurs after Awakening 'a' in Separation where the observational skills of Zazen first discern the nonfabricated voice of the Universal. The other four statements also describe key moments of development of the Resolution Sequence. Their placement defines the teaching of the intuitive mind using the symbol's embedded concepts and the grammar of awakening. The symbol illustrates progress of the relationship between the statements on intuition and the stages of the Resolution Sequence.

SUMMARY

The various forms of the Nonduality – Resolution Sequence Symbol supply practitioners with the means to study simultaneously the background concepts of the process of awakening and the experiential ground of the grammar of awakening. This is the sought-after outcome of augmenting rhetorical inquiry with the more direct and deeper symbolic method. Mastery of the material and method requires a patient period of preparation. This way may seem to bog down movement and realization. However, a sure path of coping with, and ultimately resolving conditioned states makes dealing with the initial difficulties worthwhile.

In the Appendix, we will continue the examination the effects of placing various Buddhist teachings on the symbol. Those included furnishing more examples of the universality of the symbol's composition.

Chapter 6
What Have We Learned?

*"To seek the path of Buddhahood while not knowing
the proper sequence of practice…
is like trying to put a square peg in a round hole."*[35]
Zen Master Chinhul

After a recent presentation of *Tending the Fire*, one of the attendees approached me, said some nice things about the book, and ended with a rhetorical question, "But does it work?" He left quickly before I could answer leaving the question for me to answer for myself. I suppose I wanted readers to agree with my methodology and enjoy its benefits, if not, why would I have gone through the trouble writing and publishing the text. However, during the writing process, I had only a faint hope that others might find symbols and their ability to express wide-ranging Zen concepts in graphical form a reasonable idea. The ubiquitous Enso thrives everywhere, but the steps to the generation of its symbolic wholeness remain an activity of little interest.

"Does it work?" is really two questions: "Will it work for me"? and "Has it worked for you?" The answer to the first question is easy. It works for me providing the organizational framework for practice and progress, and also a provides a place for continuing research.

The answer to the second question is a work in progress. I could not offer a meaningful response when the question was first posed. However, since then, I have verified that practitioners with a modicum of preparation benefit from the knowledge of the sequence of the process. This has been accomplished through group and individual study.

It may be that symbolic Zen is a personal skillful means, and those of similar mental inclination will find its message beneficial. Then, as in mathematics, graphical representations might gradually replace ad hoc rhetorical analysis with a universal and orderly means of a process of awakening.[36]

In Chapter 1 we posed three questions about whether or not

symbols would be effective instruments in the development of Zen awakening. No answers were attempted at that time. Now that the symbols are complete and the grammar for each established, it is possible to reflect on their potential place within the Zen educational model. We will open the gates of conjecture one at a time and look to see what pops up upon reflection.

All answers to these inquiries are envisioned and made by individuals or groups who studied the basic meanings of the Nonduality and Resolution Sequence Symbols. In other words, we will imagine these individuals or groups understand the Buddhist concepts and grammar of awakening embedded in the geometric patterns and that their responses are speculative even though they might sound definitive when read.

Before symbols gained pervasive authority in mathematics, it was a subject of great interest for a few; afterward it became a discipline of great power for many. **Can symbolizing Buddhist teachings have similar effects on Sangha development?**
If a number of individuals partake in the understanding of the symbols, they will begin to share a common language. Their grasp of the basics will set them apart, putting them in a different league by virtue of the acquired knowledge. For example, as a group they will recognize the factual existence of the Twelve Links of the Chain of Causation, as well as the experiential reality of conditioned states. The means of communication between group members will be up close and personal with no need to rehash well-defined and commonly understood issues. The evolution of the first principles sets the stage for moving together, from beginners' meditation of composure and the rudiments of tranquility and insight, to meditation devoted to the examination of the meaning of the intuitive relationship of the Personal and Universal Aspects of Mind and the nature of transformation.

Sangha development could thus advance because of the shared language that includes beginners' conceptual knowledge. The commonly held symbolic language presents a field of open-ended improvement, and because the group shares this communication skill, they share the knowledge, new insights, and most importantly within the sphere of sharing, the community-building transcendent joy of generosity. With greater numbers accepting the value of symbols over time, learning and experience in Buddhist Sanghas naturally move forward. Mathematics took many decades to realize the value of the movement from rhetorical statements to symbols. Perhaps Zen awakening will follow a similar timeline.

Could symbols simplify and facilitate the study of the Zen awakening process, removing the notion that awakening is only possible for monks and specialists who are able to dedicate their lives to its pursuit?

The pursuit of Zen awakening includes life altering transformative experiences. Many teachers do not emphasize transformation, others such as Zen Master Hakuin, speak freely and openly of the personal changes brought about in breakthroughs.[37] The Nonduality and Resolution Sequence Symbols depict the basic teachings on meditation offered by Shakyamuni Buddha, Tung-shan Liang-chieh, Dōgen Zenji, and Hakuin's teacher Shoju Ronin. Learning the contextual background for each of these teachers and their cultural modes of expression can be a daunting task for most lay practitioners. The symbols do not require this knowledge for comprehension of the connections and similarities among their teachings. With symbols as the heart of practice, the process of awakening begins and remains at the center of attention. Additional context can be added with study, widening one's outlook and understanding without clouding the primary objective.

There are two basic faults that commonly occur within Zen practice that the use of symbols acts to redress:

1) Some practitioners believe Zazen furnishes all that is necessary to cure all the cares and woes of life. John Welwood, in his book *Toward a Psychology of Awakening*, examines how people who seek awakening

sometimes attempt to sidestep the difficulties of worldly life by assuming spiritual insight will solve all their problems. Welwood calls this misguided effort "spiritual bypassing."[38] It is a common but mistaken response to the discomfort and dissatisfaction of daily life. In spiritual bypassing, problematic emotional and personal issues are left unresolved, while spiritual practices are emphasized as a way to find release from the pain associated with them. Spirituality becomes the focus through which life is judged, giving it specialness out of proportion with the fundamental needs of the individual. When we try to forge ahead without answering both our personal and spiritual needs, the result is developmental disharmony. Ultimately, we cannot avoid addressing unresolved concerns. If imbalances are not dealt with directly, they will come in the back door, usually in chaotic and destructive forms.

2) That a willful act of "letting go" brings about the resolution of conditioning even when the same mental formations repeat themselves again and again after being consciously dismissed. The myth of letting go resides in the misunderstanding that it is possible to resolve conditioned states by an act of will. Conditioned states are deeply rooted psychophysical formations. When triggered, the associated afflictive emotions manifest in painful ways. Just saying stop does not resolve the deeply rooted conditioned state; that requires a transformative experience. Transformation resolves the conditioned state and the psychophysical formation, freeing the mind and body from their negative influences. This is the foundation of Buddhist liberation.

Practitioners who take the time to learn the symbolic process of awakening facilitate meaningful and consistent efforts in line with their lives' actual needs. They minimize the chance of getting trapped by either spiritual bypassing or the myth of letting go. Symbols are compact representations of empirical experience. Understanding the grammar of awakening embodied in the symbols roots practitioners in comprehensible teachings, logic, and instructions, and especially the teachings of the relationship of dualities as complementary foci.

77

When we learn how to know both sides of every proposition, and can discern their commonalities and differences, the harmony of their relationship reveals itself. Two examples of this type of existential harmony are the liberating relationship of mental afflictions and awakening, and the creative dialogue between the Personal and Universal Aspects of Mind.

Can symbolic notation that graphically depicts the existential process of awakening come to be technically and intellectually effective as symbols are in mathematics? Symbolic notation in mathematics paves the way to the unknown of the equation; the analog in the practice of Zen is the process and experience of awakening. The symbols graphically display the features of experience, each of which contributes to a beneficial outcome. The following is a partial list of the features of experience that the symbols bring to a practitioner who has established and cultivated the study of the symbolic notation of the process of awakening.

- Organization and focus of intention
- Reduction of confusion which speeds up the process
- Understands the nature of transformation
- Capable of knowing the rate of change and degree of progress being made
- Recognition of quality and quantity of change
- Ability to communicate process to others
- Perceives the process of awakening as whole and in detail

The core Buddhist concepts plus the grammar of awakening were set piece by piece during the creation of the symbols. The following is a partial list of the teachings and grammar incorporated during the assembly process.

- Comprehensive understanding of nonduality
- Practice of Zazen
- The nature of dualities
- The relationship of nonduality and dualities
- The Triple Body of Nirmanakaya (Deconstruction),

Sambhogakaya (Reconstruction), and Dharmakaya (Unencumbered Activity)
- The four awakenings
- The difference between coping and transformation
- Nirvana as mastery of mind and cessation of suffering
- Idiosyncratic embodiment of conditioned states and how to resolve them

Can the symbols in Zen be effective as they are in mathematics? We have no way of comprehensively knowing because there are few practitioners to interview who use the symbols. Time will tell first if practitioners find them valuable, and second, whether they lead to the outcome practitioners seek. However, we can conclude that if someone has the grammar of awakening and Buddhist concepts at their fingertips, their practice will be enhanced in at least six ways:

- Capability to explain the process of awakening and how it works
- Combining grammar of awakening and the Resolution Sequence creates a strong foundation of inquiry
- Increased self-control and focused effort because of the orderliness of the methodology
- Opportunities to verify proficiency of engagement with the process of awakening
- For research into forming new skillful means and ways of exploring connections with science, philosophy, other religions, etc.
- Reduction in the possibility of becoming trapped in naïve and erroneous understandings of the process of awakening

SUMMARY

While we are unable now to answer any of these questions definitively, the chance of significant advantage appears exceedingly probable for practitioners who incorporate the symbolic way into their practice.

APPENDIX

Placing Symbols in Study and Practice

The Fourfold Dharmadhatu

Shakyamuni Buddha summarized his teaching as: "I teach the nature of *dukkha* and its cessation." In the Lankavatara Sutra, his "how to" sutra, he delineated the fundamental teaching on cessation. Later the Hua-yan philosophers of Tang Dynasty China formulated its principles into the form of the Fourfold Dharmadhatu. The Fourfold Dharmadhatu are:

- The Dharmadhatu of "phenomenon," or "form," the realm (Sanskrit: dhatu) of the Personal Aspect of Mind
- The Dharmadhatu of "noumenon" or "principle," the realm of the Universal Aspect of Mind
- The Dharmadhatu of "non-obstruction" or "harmony," the realm of the refinement of the relationship of the Universal Mind and Personal Mind
- The Dharmadhatu of the "attained unity," the realm of free interplay of the Universal and Personal Aspects of Mind

The Fourfold Dharmadhatu contains the step-by-step formula for the study and experience of the intimate relationship of the Personal (conventional, apparent, relative) and Universal (ultimate, real, absolute) Aspects of Mind within the maturation process of the Bodhisattva Way. Those who follow Buddha's instructions demonstrate its efficacy and accuracy by awakening to the truth of the cessation of *dukkha*.

The Appendix contains four views of Shakyamuni Buddha's teaching on the Fourfold Dharmadhatu, the essential teaching of Buddhist liberation from which all sectarian teachings have their root. Though the four views seem wildly divergent, at heart, they substantially conform to the Buddha's original instructions. The four views are:

- Shakyamuni Buddha's teaching on the Four Dhyanas found in the Lankavatara Sutra

- Tung-shan Liang-chieh's Soto Zen teaching on the Five Ranks
- Dogen, the Genjo Koan, and the Five Ranks
- Hakuin's teacher Shoju Rojin's instruction on the Five Ranks

Any one of them would be a basis for a lifetime study, but considering them together uncovers relationships and understandings that examination of individual views might not have brought to light. The Awakenings Chart presents the basic correlations that exist between the teachings of the Buddha and other Masters, along with teachings on awakenings from *Tending the Fire: An Introspective Guide to Zen Awakening*. Each section includes a Nonduality – Resolution Sequence Symbol augmented with that section's teaching along with explanatory information.

The Nonduality – Resolution Sequence Symbol was developed as a means to capture the existential process of the Fourfold Dharmadhatu. If one takes the time to understand the teachings illustrated by the Nonduality – Resolution Sequence Symbol, the relationships contained within the symbol, along with the added information, convey the Fourfold Dharmadhatu's central truth for each of the four views, helping to keep confusion over apparent differences to a minimum, while offering a template for coherent understanding.

THE AWAKENINGS OF THE NONDUALITY RESOLUTION
SEQUENCE SYMBOL
AND SELECTED BUDDHIST TEACHINGS

	Realm of Form Identifying Conditioned States Awakening 'a'	Realm of Principle Resolving Conditioned States Awakening 'A'	Realm of Harmony Integrating Freedom Awakening 'Aa'	Realm of Unity Living Freedom Awakening 'AA'
Shakyamuni Buddha *Four Dhyana Lankavatara Sutra*	Dhyana practiced by beginners to gain composure	Dhyana devoted to the examination of meaning	Dhyana with Thusness (*Tathata*) as its object	Dhyana of the Buddha Tathágatas
Tung-shan Liang-chieh *The Five Ranks*	The Personal within the Universal The Universal within the Personal	Coming from within the Universal	Arriving within the Personal	Attainment in both the Personal and Universal
Eihei Dōgen's Verse from the Genjo Koan *Dogen and the Five Ranks*	To study the Buddha Way is to study the self. To study the self is to forget the self.	To forget the self is to be actualized by the myriad things.	When actualized by the myriad things, your body and mind as well as the bodies and minds of others will drop away.	No trace of realization remains and this no-trace continues endlessly
Shoju Rojin *Instructions to Hakuin*	The Great Perfect Mirror Wisdom	The Universal Nature Wisdom	The Marvelous Observing Wisdom	The Perfecting-of-Action Wisdom

The Four Dhyana of Shakyamuni Buddha

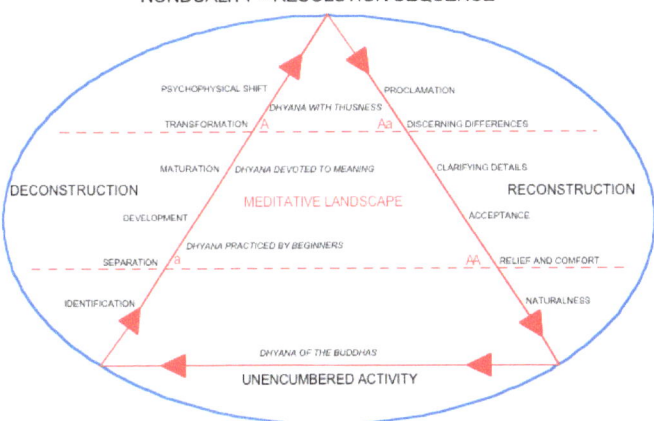

NONDUALITY – RESOLUTION SEQUENCE

PSYCHOPHYSICAL SHIFT — PROCLAMATION

DHYANA WITH THUSNESS

TRANSFORMATION — A — Aa — DISCERNING DIFFERENCES

MATURATION — DHYANA DEVOTED TO MEANING — CLARIFYING DETAILS

DECONSTRUCTION — RECONSTRUCTION

MEDITATIVE LANDSCAPE

DEVELOPMENT — ACCEPTANCE

DHYANA PRACTICED BY BEGINNERS

SEPARATION — a — AA — RELIEF AND COMFORT

IDENTIFICATION — NATURALNESS

DHYANA OF THE BUDDHAS

UNENCUMBERED ACTIVITY

ZAZEN – INTROSPECTION

The Four Dhyana (meditative concentrations) Shakyamuni Buddha elucidated in the Lankavatara Sutra are placed on the Nonduality – Resolution Sequence Symbol.

- The *Dhyana Practiced by Beginners* and *Dhyana Devoted to Meaning* are within the Meditative Landscape of Deconstruction because they are meditative concentrations that deal with learning basic principles of meditation and identifying and working with the afflictive emotions and fundamental misperceptions arising from conditioned states (Awakening 'a').
- The *Dhyana with Thusness* is in the apex of the triangle indicating a Transformation has taken place and that work in Reconstruction will follow (Awakening 'A' leading to Awakening 'Aa').
- The *Dhyana of the Buddhas* is placed in Unencumbered Activity denoting attainment of unity of action (Awakening 'AA').

Shakyamuni Buddha's Teaching on The Four Dhyana

"Transcendental Intelligence rises when the intellectual-mind
reaches its limit and,
if things are to be realized in their true and essence nature,
its processes of mentation, which are based on particularized ideas,
discriminations and judgments,
must be transcended by an appeal to some higher faculty of cognition."[39]
Shakyamuni Buddha in the Lankavatara Sutra

What follows below is an excerpt from the Lankavatara Sutra where Shakyamuni Buddha explains his teaching on the Four Dhyana: meditation of beginners, meditation on meaning, meditation on Thusness (Suchness) as its object, and the realization of Tathágatahood. The selection is from the Lankavatara Sutra chapter entitled Self-Realization. Buddha begins with his description of solitude, the foundation with which Self-realization can be explored, understood, and realized.

"'Then Mahamati asked the Blessed One, saying: 'What are the steps that will lead an awakened disciple toward the self-realization of Noble Wisdom?'

Therefore, Mahamati, let those disciples who wish to realize Noble Wisdom by following the Tathágata Vehicle desist from all discrimination and erroneous reasoning about such notions as the elements that make up the aggregates of personality and its sense-world or about such ideas as causation, rising, abiding and destruction, and exercise themselves in the discipline of Dhyana that leads to the realization of Noble Wisdom.

To practice Dhyana, earnest disciples should retire to a quiet and solitary place, remembering that life-long habits of discriminative thinking cannot be broken off easily or quickly. There are four kinds of concentrative meditation (*Dhyana*): The Dhyana practiced by the beginner; the Dhyana devoted to the examination of meaning; the

Dhyana with "Suchness" (*Tathata*) for its object; and the Dhyana of the Tathágatas.

The Dhyana practiced by the beginner is the one resorted to by those who are following the example of the disciples and masters but who do not understand its purpose and, therefore, it becomes "still-sitting" with vacant minds. This Dhyana is practiced, also, by those who see the body as a shadow and a skeleton full of suffering and impurity, and yet who cling to the notion of an ego, seek to attain emancipation by the mere cessation of thought.

The Dhyana devoted to the examination of meaning, is the one practiced by those who, perceiving the untenability of such ideas as self, other and both, which are held by the philosophers, and who have passed beyond the twofold-ego-less-ness, devote Dhyana to an examination of the significance of ego-less-ness and the differentiations of the Bodhisattvas stages.

The Dhyana with Tathata, or "Suchness", or Thusness, or Oneness, or Divine Name, for its object is practiced by those earnest disciples and masters who, while fully recognizing the twofold ego-less-ness and the imageless-ness of Tathata, yet cling to the notion of an ultimate Tathata.

The Dhyana of the Tathágatas is the Dhyana of those who are entering upon the stage of Tathágata-hood and who, abiding in the triple bliss, which characterizes the self-realization of Noble Wisdom, are devoting themselves for the sake of all beings to the accomplishment of incomprehensible works for their emancipation. This is the pure Dhyana of the Tathágatas. When all lesser things and ideas are transcended and forgotten, and there remains only a perfect state of imageless-ness where Tathágata and Tathata are merged into perfect Oneness, then the Buddhas will come together from all their Buddha-lands and with shining hands resting on his forehead will welcome a new Tathágata.'"[40]

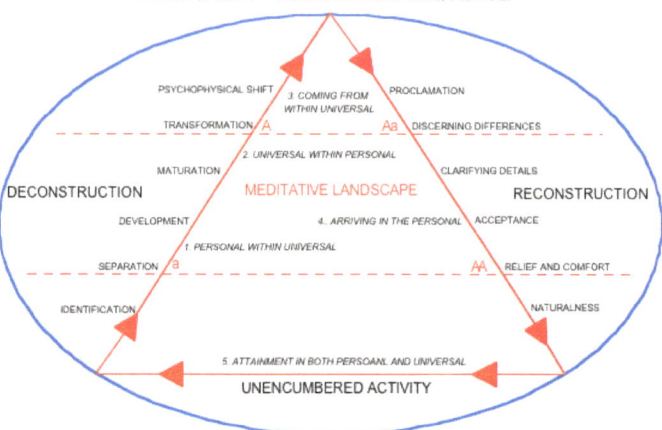

The Five Ranks of Tung-shan Liang-chieh
NONDUALITY – RESOLUTION SEQUENCE

The Five Ranks of Tung-shan Liang-chieh are added to the Nonduality – Resolution Sequence Symbol.

- The *Personal within the Universal* indicates accomplishment of Awakening 'a' and entry into Development.
- The *Universal within the Personal* is working in Maturation on conditioned states.
- *Coming from the Universal* means a Transformation has taken place (Awakening 'A').
- *Arriving in the Personal* is working on refinement of the relation of the Personal and Universal in Reconstruction (Awakening 'Aa').
- *Attainment in both Universal and Personal* is unimpeded Naturalness (Awakening 'AA').
- The fivefold spiritual body of the Five Ranks consists of 1) discipline, 2) concentration, 3) insight, 4) liberation, and 5) knowledge of the process of liberation.

The Five Ranks of
Tung-shan Liang-chieh

"Patience, knowledge, and kindness combine to comprehend the five ranks of the spiritual realm."
—The Flower Ornament Sutra

BACKGROUND

Tung-shan Liang-chieh, the founder of the Soto Zen School, promulgated the Five Ranks teaching of Zen. However, the dialectic formula of the Five Ranks might have been inspired by the I Ching, the ancient Chinese Book of Changes, and made its entry into Zen through the philosophical Hua-yan school.[41] Tung-shan Liang-chieh adapted the Five Rank's metaphysics into a practical means to teach the Buddhadharma. The Five Ranks are essentially a Chinese expression of the Indian path to awakening.

Tung-shan Liang-chieh's Five Ranks spread through the Zen Schools of China and Japan. The prominent Japanese Rinzai teacher, Hakuin, held them in high esteem and wrote a commentary on their relationship to koan practice. Dōgen outwardly rejected the formulaic and structured approach of the Five Ranks as a teaching method. However, he covertly inserted them into many areas of his writings, especially the Shobogenzo, because he understood their value in undermining deep-seated misconceptions, even though he considered systematic and academic forms inconsistent with traditional teaching methods.

THE FIVE RANKS

The terms Personal Mind and Universal Mind used below were chosen to depict the worlds of Relative and Absolute, respectively. Other studies use a variety of designations of the dualistic pair such Apparent and Real, Form and Emptiness, Difference and Unity, Individual and Collective, Diversity and Universality, etc. All of them, and others, are similar in meaning and should be considered interchangeable.

1. *The Personal Mind within the Universal Mind*: At this level the Universal, one's Original Nature, dawns within the Personal. A new way of living in the world is unveiled, one grounded in experiential observation, inquiry, and certainty.

2. *The Universal Mind within the Personal Mind*: Here the Universal is the dominant sphere acting as a container for the thoughts, feelings, and aspirations of the Personal.

3. *Coming from within the Universal*: The inconceivable mind comes to the forefront, introducing the new world of unity of the Personal and Universal. The Universal is reflected within the Personal.

4. *Arriving within the Personal*: Within this rank, the Universal and Personal beneficially interact, refining the attributes of the Personal. Each phenomenon's unique expression of the Universal is intimately perceived.

5. *Attainment in both the Personal and Universal*: Unity of the Personal and Universal is attained, so that they respond in unobstructed harmony to each other and with the world at large. Shakyamuni Buddha defined this process and relationship as, "Through intuitive-mind, by the faculty of intuition, which is a mingling of both identity and perceiving, the inconceivable wisdom of Universal Mind is revealed and made realizable." [42]

The first and second ranks prepare the mind for the third rank where the pivot point of Zen practice, the revealed Universal, penetrates and imbues life with its principle of omnipresence. The fourth rank integrates the Personal and Universal Aspects of Mind, cultivating their mutuality. The fifth rank establishes perfect freedom as the norm.

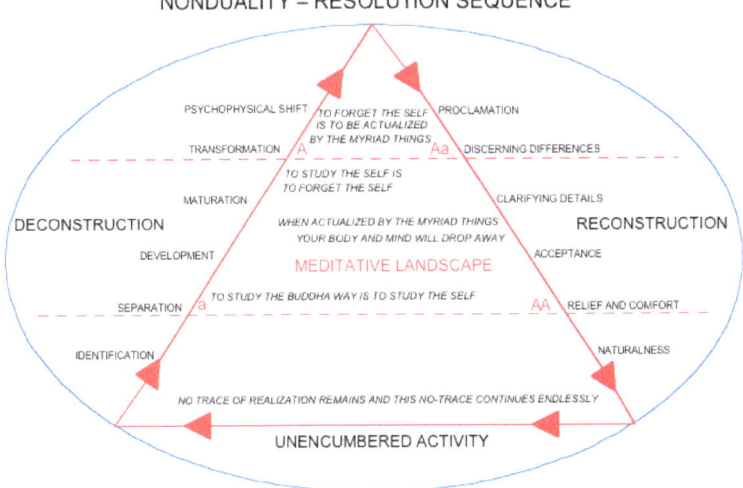

The Genjo Koan of Eihei Dogen
NONDUALITY – RESOLUTION SEQUENCE

PSYCHOPHYSICAL SHIFT — TO FORGET THE SELF IS TO BE ACTUALIZED BY THE MYRIAD THINGS — PROCLAMATION

TRANSFORMATION — A — Aa — DISCERNING DIFFERENCES

TO STUDY THE SELF IS TO FORGET THE SELF

MATURATION — CLARIFYING DETAILS

WHEN ACTUALIZED BY THE MYRIAD THINGS YOUR BODY AND MIND WILL DROP AWAY

DECONSTRUCTION — RECONSTRUCTION

DEVELOPMENT — ACCEPTANCE

MEDITATIVE LANDSCAPE

TO STUDY THE BUDDHA WAY IS TO STUDY THE SELF

SEPARATION — a — AA — RELIEF AND COMFORT

IDENTIFICATION — NATURALNESS

NO TRACE OF REALIZATION REMAINS AND THIS NO-TRACE CONTINUES ENDLESSLY

UNENCUMBERED ACTIVITY

ZAZEN – INTROSPECTION

Zen Master Dōgen's teaching from the Genjo Koan is placed on the Nonduality – Resolution Sequence Symbol.

- *To study the Buddha Way is to study the self* indicates accomplishment of Awakening 'a' and entry into Development.
- *To study the self is to forget the self* is working in Maturation on conditioned states.
- *To forget the self is to be actualized by the myriad things* means a Transformation (Awakening 'A') has taken place.
- *When actualized by the myriad things, your body and mind, as well as the bodies and minds of others will drop away* is working on refinement of the relation of the Personal and Universal Aspects of Mind in Reconstruction. (Awakening 'Aa')
- *No trace of realization remains and this no-trace continues endlessly* is unimpeded Naturalness. (Awakening 'AA')

Dōgen and the Five Ranks

"To study the Buddha Way is to study the self. To study the self is to forget the self. To forget the self is to be actualized by the myriad things. When actualized by the myriad things, your body and mind, as well as the bodies and minds of others drop away. No trace of realization exists, and this no-trace continues endlessly."[43]

Eihei Dōgen in the *Genjo Koan*

Zen Master Dōgen's famous passage on the self from the Genjo Koan quoted above unveils a broadened understanding of his introspective intent. Dōgen insists on a thorough and rigorous examination of the functioning of the self in order to overturn deeply entrenched unquestioned assumptions regarding its nature. The introspection contained in these five statements points toward a penetrating insight demonstrating how to structure the study and practice of Buddhist teachings. The five statements are an outline of Zen practice and, in a surreptitious way, mirror the Five Ranks without mentioning them by name.

The Five Ranks were promulgated in the teachings of Tung-shan Liang-chieh (807-869), the founder of the Soto Zen School. Tung-shan and his followers adapted the Five Rank's into a practical means to teach the Buddhadharma. Tung-shan's Five Ranks spread through the Zen Schools of China and Japan. The prominent Japanese Rinzai teacher Hakuin (1686-1768) held them in high esteem calling them "that supreme treasure of the Mahayana." Dōgen outwardly rejected the formulaic approach of the Five Ranks as a teaching method. However, he covertly inserted them into many areas of his writings. He probably understood their inherent value in undermining deep-seated misconceptions, but considered systematic forms to be inconsistent with his teaching of all-inclusive wholeness.

What follows is a comparison of the Five Ranks of Tung-shan and Dōgen's five statements from the Genjo Koan. A brief description of the Five Ranks will be presented first, and then the message of the five statements will be contrasted with the interpretations of the Five Ranks.

THE FIVE RANKS

The terms Personal and Universal Aspects of Mind were chosen to depict the worlds of Relative and Absolute, respectively. Other studies use a variety of designations of the dualistic pair such Apparent and Real, Form and Emptiness, Difference and Unity, Individual and Collective, Diversity and Universality, etc. All of them and others are similar in meaning and should be considered interchangeable. They describe the halves of our dualistic mind that the teaching of the Five Ranks addresses.

- Personal refers to the distinct and unique components of an individual, products of an individual's education, quality of nurturing, volitional acts, and the immediate cultural environment.
- The Universal is made up of collective and ultimate characteristics, defined as the shared action of the universe conditioning an individual's life, arising from the actions of beings presently alive and all those actions antecedent from deepest antiquity.
- The interpenetration of the Universal and Personal manifests in a complementary relationship. The Personal and Universal aspects of the self, taken together, comprise the unified structure of an individual.

The First and Second Ranks prepare the mind for the Third Rank where the pivot point of Zen practice – the fully revealed Universal – penetrates and imbues life with its principles of impermanence, interdependence, and intimacy. The Fourth Rank integrates the fully revealed Universal with the Personal, cultivating and refining the Personal's attributes, and initiates the movement toward perceptual and behavioral freedom. The Fifth Rank establishes unity of the Personal and Universal as the norm.

First Rank – The Personal Mind within the Universal Mind

At this level, the Universal dawns within the Personal. A new perspective reveals the information arising from Alaya consciousness in the form of a continuous flow of mental, emotional, and physical events. Maintaining an alert attitude of mind promotes a continuity of awareness of mental activity that protects the practitioner from identifying with ingrained habits.

The First Rank is characterized as a breakthrough of the Universal Mind (Alaya consciousness) into the Personal.

Second Rank – The Universal Mind within the Personal Mind

Here the Universal is the dominant sphere acting as a container for the thoughts, feelings, and aspirations of the Personal. The influence of the Universal becomes powerful enough to permit the practitioner to use its positive and thoroughgoing vision to overcome inherent mistrust and skepticism. Consistent and diligent application of the observational mind begins to liberate thinking from bondage imposed by condition states. Being able to articulate what is observed—a viewpoint that trusts the intuitive information that arises from contact with the previously unknown Alaya consciousness—begins the process of freeing oneself from the afflictive influences of conditioned states. This process is based on transcendent knowledge, where practitioners develop awareness of faculties of mind, consequences, the nature of relationships, and the intimacy of meditation.

The Second Rank's major realizations are the interpenetration of the sacred (noumenon) and the mundane (phenomenon), and the ability to impartially embrace the inner and outer worlds without judgment or preference.

Third Rank – Coming from within the Universal

The inconceivable mind comes compellingly to the forefront introducing the new world of fully revealed Universal. It is an intuition of something new, an outcome of an inquiry whose immediate response answers the inquirer with complete appropriateness. The accompanying transformation announces that the old way of being has passed, and now a new spiritual dimension animates one's efforts. The Universal is reflected within the Personal as its unifying force, granting language, reason, creativity, human sentiment, and ethical relations their proper and deserved places as integration proceeds.

In the Third Rank the Personal and Universal Aspects of Mind act in unending concordance in creating compassion for self and others.

Fourth Rank – Arriving within the Personal
Within this rank, the Universal and Personal beneficially interact, refining the attributes of the Personal. One attains a life of liberation when one learns how to know both sides of every proposition, discern their commonalities and differences, and to live within and admire the harmony of their mutually beneficial relationship. Harmony is learning to live a complementary relationship, liberating the person from conditioned states and their habit energies, as well as opening up new avenues for individual and social creativity.

The refined mind of complementary relationship bridges the knife-edge separation between the Fourth and Fifth Ranks.

Fifth Rank – Attainment in both the Personal and Universal
Unity of the Personal and Universal is attained, so that they act with unobstructed harmony and complementary activity with each other and the world at large. It is the middle way of Buddhism where the Personal (the mind of discrimination) and Universal (the mind of unity) manifest with equal importance.

THE GENJO KOAN'S FIVE STATEMENTS
The Fukanzazengi (Universal Recommendations for the Practice of Zazen) was Dōgen's first writing upon his return to Japan after his training in China. In it he documented the physical and mental instructions for Zazen. His succinct directions for the mental side of practice were, "Think of Not-thinking. How do you Think of Not-

thinking? – Nonthinking." These three – Thinking, Not-thinking, and Nonthinking – can be considered close equivalents of the Personal, Universal, and complementary relationship of the Five Ranks:

- Thinking arises from an individual's idiosyncratic makeup.
- The observational mind of Not-thinking advances awareness of the reality and interplay of ordinary dualistic pairs such as such as pleasure-pain, ambiguity-clarity, and confidence-insecurity, as well as dualities requiring deeper insight such as delusion-enlightenment, birth-death, or Buddhas-ordinary beings.
- Nonthinking – the wisdom mind of Nonduality – realizes and creatively partakes in the complementary association of Thinking and Not-thinking, and in all other dualities of our inherently dualistic nature.

"To study the Buddha Way is to study the self."
Dōgen intended the five statements to be understood as guides for everyday life and practice. Mere knowledge about the Buddha Way does not relieve one of suffering. Negotiating the Way in Zazen is Dōgen's "study," providing a discerning insight that promotes the ability to monitor the self in action and to gain the ability to describe its makeup and operation.

Beginning Zazen practitioners notice the impermanent and independent nature of the thinking process. Before taking up Zazen, most often they most often regarded themselves as being in control of their thoughts. However, this assumption is almost immediately compromised in Zazen practice when they begin to notice that their thoughts come and go, mostly apart from their volition and intent. They discover that their mental life consists mainly of habitual patterns of thought and affect that arise from pre-existing conditioned states. When an environmental stimulus triggers a conditioned state, the habitual response connected with that state appears within the mental landscape.

The practice of Zazen is the first step of "study" wherein the arising of the continuous flow of the mental, emotional, and physical aspects of the Thinking mind is observed. Not-thinking is the term for gaining this observational space. Not-thinking at this stage is a perspective that observes the difference between being unconsciously trapped by Thinking and being consciously aware of how thoughts appear and pass away. Not-thinking is the emergence of a new way of awareness discovered and cultivated within Zazen. The first buds of Nonthinking begin to appear within the relationship between Thinking and Not-thinking. Nonthinking is itself the experience of the world of nonduality that is produced by the complementary relationship of Thinking and Not-thinking.

"To study the self is to forget the self."

"To forget" means to penetrate to the core of the self where Not-thinking gains strength and influence. It becomes powerful enough to permit practitioners to use its positive and thoroughgoing vision to directly perceive what Tung-shan terms the non-fabricated voice of nature. Becoming able to *"forget the self"* of accumulated habits permits that voice to resound clearly. The strong Not-thinking perspective allows a vigorous and close examination of conditioned states without getting trapped by them. Not-thinking embraces the internal world without making preferential distinctions. Not-thinking is an all-encompassing attitude of mind, one that does not attempt to modify thoughts and feelings as they arise.

The *Song of the Jewel Mirror Awareness* is Tung-shan's poem that describes the process required to attain and maintain the Jewel Mirror Awareness. In it, one of the verses explains the nature of the nonfabricated voice:

> *Although it is not fabricated, it is not without speech.*
> *It is like facing a jewel mirror:*
> *Form and image behold each other.*

It is not fabricated by human agency. It has no discernible beginning or end. It also has the means to intimately communicate. When form and image behold each other, the Jewel Mirror insight of Nonthinking is the natural result.

The nonfabricated voice of Nonthinking is the outcome of the authentic relationship of dualistic pairs. It acts in us as a unified vision free of conflict.

"To forget the self is to be actualized by the myriad things."

"To be actualized by the myriad things" means a transformation has taken place within an individual. To try to make the world conform to oneself is hopeless, painful and disappointing; when the "myriad things" manifest freely one's life is fulfilling, stimulating, and satisfying.

One of the most difficult tasks is learning to trust the source and content of information that arises from within the relationship of Thinking and Not-thinking. The beneficent activity of the universe lies beyond doubt within an accepting trust based on experiential understanding. *"To forget the self"* establishes an open and intimate relationship between the individual's life of Thinking and the *"myriad things"* of Not-thinking.

The transcendent meditation of Nonthinking acts in the spiritual realm where myriad beings exist.

"When actualized by the myriad things, your body and mind, as well as the bodies and minds of others, will drop away."

"Body and mind ... will drop away" occurs when freedom replaces conditioning. The *"myriad things"* inform and refine the intellect, emotions, speech, reason, intuition, and physical form. An abiding sense of accomplishment replaces the ascendancy of mental obscurations. One gains the capability to recognize, accept, and take pleasure in the joy of freedom. The dropping of body and mind of self and others consciously cultivates and integrates the experience of freedom.

The dualistic pair of Thinking and Not-thinking is seen to be, and always has been a creative complement communicating with the same intimate relationship that takes place between a master and disciple. This intimate communication is Nonthinking itself.

"No trace of realization remains, and this no-trace continues endlessly."

Effortless living is at the heart of *"no-trace realization." "No-trace"* means to fully engage with the world liberated from the unceasing demands of the self. In the Genjo Koan, Dōgen asserts that enlightenment exists when the self is pervious to the myriad beings and events of the world. Delusion insists the world match the needs of an individual's assumptions; enlightenment opens the self to the free activity with myriad beings. Upon attainment of unity, one becomes truly ordinary.

THE FIVE STATEMENTS AND THE FIVE RANKS

Dōgen's statements and the Five Ranks refer to the heart of Zen practice – how to relieve the mental afflictions of conditioned states by cultivation of an internal dialogue ultimately leading to nirvana or liberation. The Five Statements and the Five Ranks are both prescriptions for making freedom an actuality in one's life. The following is a descriptive summary of the progression of the awakening process.

Establishing the Relationship

"To study the Buddha Way is to study the self." – The Personal Mind within the Universal Mind

A change of perspective, Awakening 'a' is produced within Zazen practice, and it transforms one's worldview from mundane only to witnessing the sacred.

Principles of the Relationship

"To study the self is to forget the self." – The Universal Mind within the Personal Mind

A transformative change of being, Awakening 'A' creates the

understanding of compassion for self and others based on a deep intuitive understanding of the absolute equality and intimate connection of all beings.

Entering into the Relationship

"To forget the self is to be actualized by the myriad things." – Coming from within the Universal

A change of perspective, Awakening 'Aa' engages the power of empathetic concern that opens the gateway to all beings and all worlds everywhere.

Cultivating the Relationship

"When actualized by the myriad things, your body and mind, as well as the bodies and minds of others, will drop away." – Arriving within the Personal

A transformative change of behavior, Awakening 'AA' attains the view that the Personal and Universal Aspects of Mind are inseparable, equal, and engaged in intimate and unending relations.

Living the Relationship

No trace of realization remains and this no-trace continues endlessly. – Attainment in both the Personal and Universal

Wisdom and caring impulses arise continuously, bestowed like a gift. The *Brahma Viharas* of kindness, compassion, nonspecific gratitude, and intimacy express themselves effortlessly in small and grand ways.

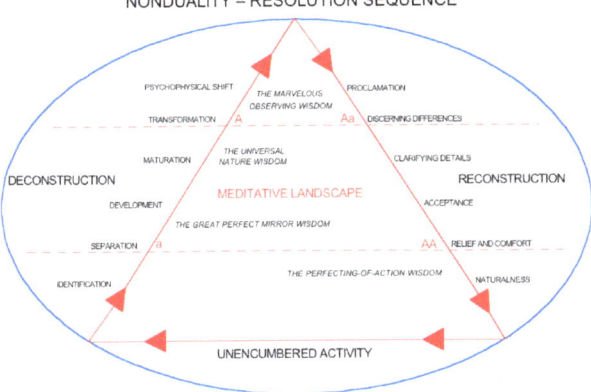

Shoju Ronin's Instructions to Hakuin

NONDUALITY – RESOLUTION SEQUENCE

PSYCHOPHYSICAL SHIFT

THE MARVELOUS OBSERVING WISDOM

PROCLAMATION

TRANSFORMATION   A   Aa   DISCERNING DIFFERENCES

THE UNIVERSAL NATURE WISDOM

CLARIFYING DETAILS

MATURATION

DECONSTRUCTION   RECONSTRUCTION

MEDITATIVE LANDSCAPE

DEVELOPMENT   ACCEPTANCE

THE GREAT PERFECT MIRROR WISDOM

SEPARATION   a   AA   RELIEF AND COMFORT

THE PERFECTING-OF-ACTION WISDOM

IDENTIFICATION   NATURALNESS

UNENCUMBERED ACTIVITY

ZAZEN – INTROSPECTION

The Wisdom meditations of Shoju Ronin describe the awakenings of the Nonduality – Resolution Sequence Symbol.

- The *Great Perfect Mirror Wisdom* and the *Universal Nature Wisdom* are placed within the Meditative Landscape of Deconstruction because they are meditative concentrations that deal with learning basic principles of meditation and with identifying and working with the afflictive emotions of conditioned states (Awakening 'a').

- The *Marvelous Observing Wisdom* is in apex of the triangle indicating a Transformation has taken place and that work in Reconstruction will follow (Awakening 'A' leading to Awakening 'Aa').

- The *Perfecting-of-Action Wisdom* is placed in Unencumbered Activity denoting attainment of unity of action (Awakening 'AA').

Zen Master Hakuin's Time with His Teacher Shoju Ronin

Zen Master Hakuin Ekaku (1686-1768) was instrumental in reviving Japanese Rinzai Zen from a long decline through his untiring insistence on plumbing the depths of experience and generously sharing the results in teaching, art, and writings. He left Dharma heirs of character and experience who continued his work of revitalization and transformation. He also produced marvelous paintings of Buddhist folklore, well- known Buddhist teachers, and many self-portraits, as well as volumes of Zen instructions, narratives, and his famous autobiography *Wild Ivy*. Every Zen student should have a copy on his or her bedside bookshelf.

Hakuin wrote *Wild Ivy* when he was in his eighties, and it covers the first thirty years of his life. His motivation, like most everything in his life, was to offer inspiration and instruction, putting forth the strength of his approach to koan introspection. He recounts his early years as a child, young monk, and seeker of clarification of awakenings experienced during his youth. He sought to polish and expand his insight. Through a fellow student, Hakuin heard of a well-respected teacher named Shoju. He traveled to Shoju's temple and was accepted, practicing with him for eight tumultuous, life-defining months. Leaving after a major breakthrough, Hakuin expressed abiding gratitude, praising Shoju's teaching ability and regard for the well-being of his students.

The Wisdom Meditations of Shoju roughly convey the awakenings of The Nonduality – Resolution Sequence Symbol, showing how the Five Ranks and the Three Bodies (Nirmanakaya – Deconstruction, Sambhogakaya – Reconstruction, Dharmakaya – Unencumbered Activity) are integral to the symbol. His brief teaching clearly expounds understanding of their relationship, occupying the key position in the process of awakening.

Hakuin's *Keiso Dokuzi* goes over the same ground of the Five Ranks, using Tung-shan's Song of the Jewel Mirror Awareness verses to communicate clearly the "reciprocal interpenetration." Without the Five Ranks, students remain outsiders until they enter the real universe where Personal and Universal interpenetrate. Hakuin's voice doesn't hold back, singing the praises of the Dharma. "How vast is the heaven of boundless samadhi! How bright and transparent the moonlight of wisdom!"

Shoju Ronin gave Hakuin the gift of the Five Ranks. Without attainment of them and the Four Wisdom Meditations, Hakuin echoes Shoju we cannot call ourselves Sons or Daughters of Buddha. The awakenings of the symbol in their own way point the light on the Five Ranks, the Four Wisdoms, and the Three Bodies.

Shoju Ronin's Summary Instructions to Hakuin on the Five Ranks, the Four Wisdoms, and the Three Bodies

What is there outside us, what is there we lack?
Nirvana is openly shown to our eyes.
This earth where we stand is the pure lotus-land,
and this very body, the body of Buddha.
—From Master Hakuin's *Song in Praise of Zazen*

Shoju Ronin has said, "In order to provide a means whereby students might directly experience the Four Wisdoms the patriarchs, in their compassion and with their skill in devising expedients, first instituted the Five Ranks." What are the so-called Four Wisdoms? They are:

- The Great Perfect Mirror Wisdom
- The Universal Nature Wisdom
- The Marvelous Observing Wisdom
- The Perfecting-of-Action Wisdom

"Followers of the Way, even though you may have pursued your studies in the Threefold Learning continuously through many kalpas, if you have not directly experienced the Four Wisdoms, you are not permitted to call yourselves true sons or daughters of Buddha.

FIRST WISDOM

Followers of the way, if your investigation has been correct and complete, at the moment you smash open the dark cave of the eighth or Alaya consciousness, the precious light of the 'Great Perfect Mirror Wisdom' instantly shines forth.

But, strange to say, the light of the 'Great Perfect Mirror Wisdom' is black like lacquer. This is what is called the rank of 'The Apparent within the Real.' *[The Personal within the Universal]*

SECOND WISDOM

Having attained the Great Perfect Mirror Wisdom, you now enter the rank of 'The Real within the Apparent.' *[The Universal within the Personal]* When you have accomplished your long practice of the jeweled-mirror Samadhi, you directly realize 'Universal Nature Wisdom' and for the first time enter the state of the unobstructed inter-penetration of noumenon and phenomena. But the disciple must not be satisfied here. He himself must enter into intimate acquaintance with the rank of 'The Coming from within the Real.' *[Coming from within the Universal]*

THIRD WISDOM

After that, by depending upon the rank of 'The Arrival at Mutual Integration,' *[Arriving within the Personal]* he will completely prove the 'Marvelous Observing Wisdom.'

FOURTH WISDOM

With 'Perfecting-of-Action Wisdom' at last one reaches the rank of 'Unity Attained,'*[Attainment in both the Personal and Universal]* and, after all, comes back to sit among the coals and ashes.

Do you know why? Pure gold that has gone through a thousand smeltings does not become ore a second time. My only fear is that a little gain will suffice you. How priceless is the merit gained through the step-by-step practice of the Five Ranks of the Apparent and the Real! *[Personal and Universal]* By this practice you not only attain the Four Wisdoms, but you personally prove that the Three Bodies also are wholly embraced within your own body.

Have you not read in the Daijo Shogongyo Ron:
'When the eight consciousnesses are inverted, the Four Wisdoms are produced; when the Four Wisdoms are bound together, the Three Bodies are perfected?'

Therefore, Sokei Daishi composed this verse:

'Your own nature is provided
With the Three Bodies;
When its brightness is manifested,
The Four Wisdoms are attained.'

Sokei Daishi also said:

The pure Dharmakaya (Body of Truth) is your nature;
The perfect Sambhogakaya (Body of Refinement and Enjoyment) is your wisdom;
The myriad Nirmanakayas (Body of Manifestation and Transformation) are
your activities.'''

The Keiso Dokuzi

The Five Ranks of The Apparent (Personal) and the Real (Universal):
By Hakuin Zenji

We do not know by whom the Jeweled-mirror Samadhi was composed. From Sekito Osho, Yakusan Osho, and Ungan Osho, it was transmitted from master to master and handed down within the secret room. Never have [its teachings] been willingly disclosed until now. After it had been transmitted to Tozan Osho (Tung-shan), he made clear the gradations of the Five Ranks within it, and composed a verse for each rank, in order to bring out the main principle of Buddhism. Surely the Five Ranks is a torch on the midnight road, a ferryboat at the riverside when one has lost one's way!

But alas! The Zen gardens of recent times are desolate and barren. "Directly-pointing-to-the-ultimate" Zen is regarded as nothing but benightedness and foolishness; and that supreme treasure of the Mahayana, the Jeweled Mirror Samadhi's Five Ranks of the Apparent *[Personal]* and the Real *[Universal]*, is considered to be only the old and broken vessel of an antiquated house. No one pays any attention to it. [Today's students] are like blind men who have thrown away their staffs, calling them useless baggage. Of themselves they stumble and fall into the mud of heterodox views and cannot get out until death overtakes them. They never know that the Five Ranks is the ship that carries them across the poisonous sea surrounding the rank of the Real, the precious wheel that demolishes the impregnable prison-house of the two voids. They do not know the important road of progressive practice; they are not versed in the secret meaning within this teaching. Therefore, they sink into the stagnant water of sravaka-hood or pratyeka-buddhahood. They fall into the black pit of withered sprouts and decayed seeds. Even the hand of Buddha would find it difficult to save them.

That into which I was initiated forty years ago in the room of

Shoju I shall now dispense as the alms giving of Dharma. When I find a superior person who is studying the true and profound teaching and has experienced the Great Death, I shall give this secret transmission to him, since it was not designed for men of medium and lesser ability. Take heed and do not treat it lightly!

How vast is the heaven of boundless samadhi! How bright and transparent the moonlight of wisdom! Among these, to be sure, are a number of doctrines and orally transmitted secret teachings, yet never have I seen anything to equal the perversion of the Five Ranks, the carping criticism, the tortuous explanations, the adding of branch to branch, the piling up of entanglement upon entanglement. The truth is that the teachers who are guilty of this do not know for what principle the Five Ranks was instituted. Hence, they confuse and bewilder their students to the point that even a Sariputra or an Ananda would find it difficult to judge correctly.

Or, could it be that our patriarchs delivered themselves of these absurd ties in order to harass their posterity unnecessarily? For a long time, I wondered about this. But, when I came to enter the room of Shoju, the rhinoceros of my previous doubt suddenly fell down dead... Do not look with suspicion upon the Five Ranks, saying that it is not the directly transmitted oral teaching of the Tozan line. You should know that it was only after he had completed his investigation of Tozan's Verses that Shoju gave his acknowledgment to the Five Ranks

After I had entered Shoju's room and received transmission from him, I was quite satisfied. But though I was satisfied, I still regretted that all teachers had not yet clearly explained the meaning of " the reciprocal interpenetration of the Apparent and the Real." They seemed to have discarded the words "reciprocal interpenetration," and to pay no attention whatsoever to them. Thereupon the rhinoceros of doubt once more raised its head.

In the summer of the first year of the Kan'en era (1748-1751), in the midst of my meditation, suddenly the mystery of "the reciprocal interpenetration of the Apparent and the Real " became perfectly clear. It was just like looking at the palm of my own hand. The rhinoceros of doubt instantly fell down dead, and I could scarcely bear the joy of it. Though I wished to hand it on to others, I was ashamed to squeeze out my old woman's stinking milk and soil the monk's mouths with it.

All of you who wish to plumb this deep source must make the investigation in secret with your entire body. My own toil has extended over these thirty years. Do not take this to be an easy task! Even if you should happen to break up the family and scatter the household, do not consider this enough. You must vow to pass through seven, or eight, or even nine thickets of brambles. And, when you have passed through the thickets of brambles, still do not consider this to be enough. Vow to investigate the secret teachings of the Five Ranks to the end.

For the past eight or nine years or more, I have been trying to incite all of you who boil your daily gruel over the same fire with me to study this great matter thoroughly, but more often than not you have taken it to be the doctrine of another house, and remained indifferent to it. Only a few among you have attained understanding of it. How deeply this grieves me! Have you never heard: " The Gates of Dharma are manifold; I vow to enter them all?" How much the more should this be true for the main principle of Buddhism and the essential road of Sanzen!

ENDNOTES

[1] Dwight Goddard, *Lankavatara Sutra Epitomized Version*, p. 35

[2] Ibid, p. 9

[3] Yogacara Buddhism recognizes the storehouse consciousness (Alayavijñāna) as the eighth level of consciousnesses. The first seven are sight, sound, taste, touch, smell, consciousness, and manas. The first seven arise from within and are functions of Alayavijñāna. The storehouse Alayavijñāna acts as a storage place of the seeds of karma from which they are brought to fruition when triggered by causes and conditions.

[4] See Dale and Barbara Verkuilen, *Tending the Fire: An Introspective Guide to Zen Awakening* [Madison WI Firethroat Press 2011, pp. 3-5, pp. 39-68, and pp. 119-161] for detailed information on the Resolution Sequence, Metaphor Awareness, David Grove, and his teaching. Also see the essay in the appendix on Metaphor Awareness and Zen Meditation: A Contemporary Natural Koan Practice

[5] A copy of Dwight Goddard's epitomized translation of the Lankavatara Sutra is available at firethroatpress.com in the study guide section. All quotations from the Lankavatara Sutra in this book are taken from this re-formatted translation.

[6] Dwight Goddard, *Lankavatara Sutra Epitomized Version*, p. 45

[7] Dale and Barbara Verkuilen, *Tending the Fire: An Introspective Guide to Zen Awakening* [Madison WI Firethroat Press 2011, p. 13]

[8] Ibid, p.14

[9] E.T. Bell, *The Development of Mathematics* [New York: Dover Press, 1945, p.125]

[10] Ibid, p.120

[11] Joseph Mazur, *Enlightening Symbols* [Princeton NJ: Princeton University Press, 2014, pp. 95-96]

[12] Ibid, p. 164

[13] Ibid, p. 166-167

[14] Dwight Goddard, *Lankavatara Sutra Epitomized Version*, p. 38

[15] Ibid, p. 53

[16] Joseph Mazur, *Enlightening Symbols* [Princeton NJ: Princeton University Press, 2014, p. *x*]

[17] Dwight Goddard, *Lankavatara Sutra Epitomized Version*, p. 35

[18] Ibid, p.12

[19] Ibid, p. 30

[20] Ibid, p. 48

[21] Ibid, p. 47

[22] Gudo Nishijima's introduction to *Mitsugo* (Secret Talk) of Dōgen's Shobogenzo Fascicle #51. [Charleston, SC: BooksurgeLLC, 2005 p. 79]

[23] Ibid, p. 73

[24] Dwight Goddard, *Lankavatara Sutra Epitomized Version*, p. 26

[25] Ibid, p. 31

[26] Ibid, p. 43

[27] Ibid, p. 51

[28] Walpola Rahula, *What the Buddha Taught* [New York: Grove Press, 1959, pp. 68-69]

[29] Dwight Goddard, *Lankavatara Sutra Epitomized Version*, p. 52

[30] Dale and Barbara Verkuilen, *Tending the Fire: An Introspective Guide to Zen Awakening* [Madison WI Firethroat Press 2011 p. 59]

[31] Dwight Goddard, *Lankavatara Sutra Epitomized Version*, p. 23

[32] Francesca Freemantle, *Luminous Emptiness* [Boston: Shambala Publications, 2001 p. 37]

[33] Dwight Goddard, *Lankavatara Sutra Epitomized Version*, p. 55

[34] Joseph Mazur, *Enlightening Symbols* [Princeton NJ: Princeton University

[35] Robert Buswell, *Tracing Back the Radiance*, [Hawai'i: Kuroda Institute, 1991, p. 102]

[36] See *Zongmi on Chan* by Jeffrey Lyle Boughton for a Chinese Hua-yan and Zen Master's understanding of the process of awakening.

[37] See Hakuin's Keiso Dokuzi in the Appendix

[38] John Welwood, *Toward a Psychology of Awakening* [Boston & London: Shambala, 2000, pp. 12-13

[39] Dwight Goddard, *Lankavatara Sutra Epitomized Version*, p. 43

[40] Ibid, pp. 46-48

[41] See Sheng Yen, *The Infinite Mirror* [Boston: Shambala, 2006 pp. 103-110] for an introduction to how the Five Ranks arise from Hexagram #30 Li of the I Ching. If Master Sheng Yen is correct in his analysis, the Five Ranks can then be understood to predate Buddhism in China, and adapted by Buddhists to explain the awakening process.

[42] Dwight Goddard, *Lankavatara Sutra Epitomized Version*, p. 35

[43] Eihei Dogen translated by Kazuaki Tanahashi, *Enlightenment Unfolds* [Boston: Shambala, 2000, p. 70]

BIBLIOGRAPHY

Abram, David. *The Spell of the Sensuous*. Toronto: Random House, 1996.

Aitken, Robert. *Original Dwelling Place*. Washington D.C.: Counterpoint, 1996.

Allione, Tsultrim. *Feeding Your Demons: Ancient Wisdom For Resolving Inner Conflict*. New York: Little, Brown and Company, 2008

Bellos, Alex. *Here's Looking at Euclid*. New York: Simon & Schuster, Inc., 2010

Bielefeldt, Carl. *Dogen's Manuals of Zen Meditation*. Berkeley: University of California Press, 1988.

Chang, Garma C. C., *The Hundred Thousand Songs of Milarepa*. Boston: Shambala, 1999.

Cleary, Thomas. *Secrets of the Blue Cliff Record*. Boston: Shambala, 2000.

————. *The Secret of the Golden Flower*. New York: HarperSanFrancisco, 1991.

————. *Zen Lessons*. Boston: Shambala, 1989.

————. *The Flower Ornament Scripture*: Boston: Shambala, 1984

Cook, Francis. *Hua-yan Buddhism*. London: The Pennsylvania State Press, 1977.

————. *Sounds of Valley Streams: Translation of Nine Essays from Shobogenzo*. Albany, New York: State University of New York Press, 1989

Dumoulin, Heinrich. *Zen Buddhism: A History, India and China*. New York: Macmillan, 1994.

————. *Zen Buddhism: A History, Japan*. New York: MacMillan, 1990.

Ferguson, Andy. *Zen's Chinese Heritage*. Somerville, MA: Wisdom, 2000.

Fremantle, Francesca. *Luminous Emptiness*. Boston: Shambala, 2001.

Green, J. *The Recorded Sayings of Zen Master Joshu*. Boston: Shambala, 1998.

Goddard, Dwight. *A Buddhist Bible.* Self published 1932

Grove, David. *Training Module 1: In the Presence of the Past.* David Grove Seminars

————. *Training Module 2: Reweaving A Companionable Past.* David Grove Seminars

————. *Training Module 3: And Death Shall Have No Dominion.* David Grove Seminars

Hagen, Steve. *Buddhism Plain and Simple.* New York: HarperCollins, 1999.

Heine, Steve. *The Zen Poetry of Dogen.* Boston: Tuttle, 1997.

Hixon, Lex. *Living Buddha Zen.* Burdet. N. Y.: Larsen Publications, 1995.

Hsing Yun. *Core Ideas.* New York: Weatherhill, 2002.

————. *Lotus in a Stream.* New York: Weatherhill, 2000.

————. *Describing the Indescribable.* Somerville, MA: Wisdom, 2001.

Johnson, Will. *The Posture of Meditation.* Boston: Shambala, 1996.

Katagiri, Dainin. *Returning to Silence.* Boston: Shambala, 1988.

————. *Each Moment is the Universe.* Boston: Shambala, 2007.

Kennet, Jiyu. *How to Grow a Lotus Blossom or How a Zen Buddhist Prepares for Death.* Mt. Shasta, California: Shasta Abbey, 1993

Kim, Hee-Jin. *Dogen on Meditation and Thinking.* Albany, N.Y., SUNY Press, 2007.

Lawley, James and Penny Tompkins. *Metaphors in Mind: Transformation Through Symbolic Modeling.* London: The Developing Company Press, 2000

Leighton, Taigen and Okumura Shohaku. *Eihei Koroku.* Boston: Wisdom Publications, 2004.

————. *The Whole Hearted Way.* Boston: Tuttle, 1997.

Loori, John Daido. *Sitting with Koans.* Boston: Wisdom Publications, 2006

————. *The Art of Just Sitting: Essential Writings on the Zen Practice of Shikantaza.* Boston: Wisdom Publications, 2002

————. *The True Dharma Eye: Zen Master Dogen's Three Hundred Koans.* Boston & London: Shambhala, 2005

Low, Albert. *The Butterfly's Dream.* Boston: Tuttle, 1993.

Loy, David. *Nonduality: A Study In Comparative Philosophy*. Amherst, New York: Humanity Books an imprint of Prometheus Books, 1988

Mazur, Joseph, *Enlightening Symbols* Princeton NJ: Princeton University Press, 2014

Matsuoka, Soyu. *The Kyosaku*. Atlanta: Atlanta Soto Zen Center, 2006.

Mu Soeng. *Trust in Mind*. Boston: Wisdom Publications, 2004.

Nishijima, Gudo & Chodo Cross. *Master Dogen's Shobogenzo: Book 1*. Charleston, South Carolina: BookSurge, LLC, 1996

——————.*Master Dogen's Shobogenzo: Book 2*. Charleston, South Carolina: BookSurge, LLC, 1996

——————.*Master Dogen's Shobogenzo: Book 3*. Charleston, South Carolina: BookSurge, LLC, 1997

——————.*Master Dogen's Shobogenzo: Book 4*. Charleston, South Carolina: BookSurge, LLC, 1999

Pine, Red. *The Zen Teachings of Bodhidharma*. New York: North Point Press, 1989.

Popper, Karl. *The Open Society and its Enemies*. Princeton, N. J.: Princeton University Press, 1962.

Powell, William. *The Record of Tung-Shan*. Honolulu: Kuroda Institute, 1986.

Price, A. *The Sutra of Huineng*. Berkeley, CA: Shambala, 1975.

Rahula, Walpola. *What the Buddha Taught*. New York: Grove Press, 1959.

Shaku, Soyen. *Zen for Americans*. La Salle, IL: Open Court, 1906.

Sheng Yen. *Infinite Mirror*. Boston, MA: Shambala, 1990.

Stapp, Henry. *Mindful Universe: Quantum Mechanics and the Participating Observer*. New York: Springer, 2007.

Stryk, Lucien. *Encounters with Zen*. Athens, OH: Swallow Press, 1981.

Sullivan, Wendy and Judy Rees. *Clean Language: Revealing Metaphors and Opening Minds*. Wales, UK & Bethel, CT: Crown House Publishing Limited, 2008

Suzuki, Shunryu. *Zen Mind, Beginner's Mind*. New York: Weatherhill, 1970

Tanahashi, Kazuaki. *Enlightenment Unfolds*. Boston: Shambala, 1999.

————. *Moon in a Dew Drop*. San Francisco: North Point Press, 1985.

Verkuilen, Dale and Barbara. *Tending the Fire: An Introspective Guide to Zen Awakening*. Madison, WI: Firethroat Press, 2012.

————. *Unfolding the Eightfold Path: A Contemporary Zen Perspective*. Madison WI: Firethroat Press

Von Durckheim, Karlfried. *Hara*. London: Unwin Paperbacks, 1962.

Welwood, John. *Toward a Psychology of Awakening*. Boston: Shambala, 2000.

Taizen Dale Verkuilen has been studying Zen Buddhism since 1968 with Soyu Matsuoka Roshi, Dainin Katagiri Roshi, and Shoken Winecoff Roshi, He and his wife, Renshin Barbara, also a Zen priest, founded the Midwest Soto Zen Community in Madison, Wisconsin in 2001. His writings include *The Eightfold Path: A Contemporary Zen Perspective,* and *Tending the Fire: An Introspective Guide to Zen Awakening,* co-authored with Renshin, *Symbols and Zen: Portraying the Process of Awakening,* and a number study guide booklets.

www.ingramcontent.com/pod-product-compliance
Lightning Source LLC
Chambersburg PA
CBHW051632120626
46551CB00014B/2050